Laughter

THE BEST
MEDICINE®

Laughter

THE BEST
MEDICINE®

A Laugh-Out-Loud
Collection of our
Funniest Jokes,
Quotes, Stories
& Cartoons

Reader's
Digest

The Reader's Digest Association, Inc.
Pleasantville, NY/ Montreal

ISBN 978-0-89577-977-9

PROJECT STAFF
Editor: Deborah DeFord
Art Editor: Pegi Goodman
Research Editor: Mark LaFlaur

READER'S DIGEST TRADE PUBLISHING
Associate Art Director: George McKeon
Executive Editor, Trade Publishing: Dolores York
Manufacturing Manager: Gillian Sylvain
Vice President, U.S. Operations: Michael Braunschweiger
Associate Publisher: Rosanne McManus
President and Publisher, Trade Publishing: Harold Clarke

Previously published in 1997 as *Laughter, the Best Medicine*
(ISBN 0-89577-977-3)

Cover illustration: Travis Foster

The credits that appear on page 216 are hereby made a part of this
copyright page.

We are committed to both the quality of our products and the service we provide to
our customers. We value your comments, so please feel free to contact us.

The Reader's Digest Association, Inc.
Adult Trade Publishing
Reader's Digest Road
Pleasantville, NY 10570-7000

For more Reader's Digest products and information, visit our website:
www.rd.com

Printed in the United States

7 9 10 8

A Note from the Editors

What's your handicap these days?" one golfer asked his companion.

"I'm a scratch golfer . . . I write down all my good scores and scratch out all my bad ones."

So relates Charles Schulz, the much-loved creator of the comic strip, *Peanuts*. Schulz is just one of the many funny folks, both professional and everyday, whose jokes appear in *Laughter, The Best Medicine*®, this year celebrating 50 years of monthly funny business in *Reader's Digest*. It is the column's vast supply of homey humor that supplied this book with an unbeatable collection.

What has made *Laughter, The Best Medicine* so popular for so long? In part, the answer lies in the department's consistent ability to pinpoint — and poke fun at — the facts and foibles of daily life. Nothing is sacred — from politics, religion, technology, doctors and lawyers, to sports, pets, children, and relationships. Add to this the quality of contributors — professional comedians, joke writers, and best of all, readers themselves — and you have a winning, winsome feature that readers look forward to month after month.

You can tell a lot about people and their times by what makes them laugh. A look through 50 years of *Laughter, The Best Medicine* offers us a glimpse of the past while tickling us in the present. Remember when knock-knock jokes were the rage? How about riddles and puns? Today's hot commodities in the humor department tend to be top ten lists and computer comedy.

While there is much more to The Digest than its jokes, its regular offerings of comic relief serve a noble and delightful purpose that has been captured in this book. Letters of thanks pour in weekly from readers who rely on *Laughter, The Best Medicine* to lift their spirits, put a twinkle in their eye or simply call up a chuckle or two after a hard day at home or the office, working or watching the kids. As you take a break from your daily business, browse through the following pages and prepare for a treat. We think you'll find that, after all is said and done, laughter really is the best medicine.

—*The Editors*

Contents

"Oh, Richard, the possibilities."

People

Courting Troubles

A man is taking a woman home from their first date, and he asks if he can come inside. "Oh, no," she says. "I never ask a guy in on the first date."

"Okay," the man replies, "how about the last date?"

—HEIDI MOSELEY

Tammy: "I'm not looking to get involved with one particular guy right now, Al."

Al: "Well, luckily for you, Tammy, I'm not exactly known for being particular."

—J. C. DUFFY, Universal Press Syndicate

Mother to daughter: "What kind of a person is your new friend? Is he respectable?"

"Of course he is, Mum. He's thrifty, doesn't drink or smoke, has a very steady wife and three well-behaved children."

—LEA BERNER

How was your date last night, Billy?" his friend asked.

"Fabulous. We went to the concert, had a bite to eat, and then we drove around for a while until I found a nice dark spot to park. I asked her for a kiss, and she said that first I'd have to put the top down on the car. So I worked for an hour getting the top down—"

"An hour?" interrupted his pal. "I can put my top down in three minutes."

"I know," said Billy. "But you have a convertible."

—PHIL HARTMAN in *Ohio Motorist*

"Who said anything about marriage? What I'm offering is an array of mutual funds, variable annuities and life insurance."

While riding a bus, I overheard one woman ask another, with great curiosity, "Well, what happened on your date with dashing Prince Lancelot?"

"Yuk!" was the disillusioned reply. "He was more like disgusting Prince Lust-a-lot—and I was the one who needed the suit of armor!"

—T. HOWIE

A college friend was going to meet a young lady he knew.
"An old flame?" I asked.
He winked and said, "More like an unlit match."

—MICHAEL HARTLAND

● ●

A bachelor, just turned 40, began feeling desperate. "I went to a singles bar," he told a friend, "walked over to this 20-year-old woman and asked, 'Where have you been all my life?' She said, 'Teething.' "

—MACK McGINNIS in *Quote*

Professor to a student: "Can you think of a solution to end unemployment?"

"Yes, sir! I'd put all the men on one island and the women on another."

"And what would they be doing then?"

"Building boats!"

—SOMEN GUHA

To impress his date, the young man took her to a very chic Italian restaurant. After sipping some fine wine, he picked up the menu and ordered. "We'll have the *Giuseppe Spomdalucci*," he said.

"Sorry, sir," said the waiter. "That's the proprietor."

—JIM STARK

I'm not saying her fiancé is cheap," whispered the office gossip. "But every time I get close to her engagement ring, I have an overwhelming desire for some Cracker Jack."

—Quoted by JAMES DENT in the Charleston, W.Va., *Gazette*

She answered the phone to hear a repentant voice. "I'm sorry, darling," he said. "I have thought things over and you *can* have the Rolls-Royce as a wedding present, we *will* move to the Gold Coast, and your mother *can* stay with us. Now will you marry me?"

"Of course I will," she said. "And who is this speaking?"

—*The Rotarian*

Striking up a conversation with the attractive woman seated beside him on a coast-to-coast flight, a would-be Romeo asked, "What kind of man attracts you?"

"I've always been drawn to Native American men," she replied. "They're in harmony with nature."

"I see," said the man, nodding.

"But, then, I really go for Jewish men who put women on a pedestal, and I can rarely resist the way Southern gentlemen always treat their ladies with respect."

"Please allow me to introduce myself," said the man. "My name is Tecumseh Goldstein, but all my friends call me Bubba."

—MATTHEW W. BOYLE

Donna: "He's so romantic. Every time he speaks to me he starts with, 'Fair lady.'"

Tina: "Romantic, my eye. He used to be a bus driver."

—STEVE JENKS

What am I supposed to do?" a young man looking to get married asked his friend. "Every woman I bring home to meet my parents, my mother doesn't like."

"Oh, that's easy," his pal replied. "All you have to do is find someone who's just like your mother."

"I did that already," he said, "and that one my father didn't like."

—MINNIE HERMAN

A bachelor asked the computer to find him the perfect mate: "I want a companion who is small and cute, loves water sports, and enjoys group activities."

Back came the answer: "Marry a penguin."

—Rainbow

• •

An 85-year-old widow went on a blind date with a 90-year-old man. When she returned to her daughter's house later that night, she seemed upset. "What happened, Mother?" the daughter asked.

"I had to slap his face three times!"

"You mean he got fresh?"

"No," she answered. "I thought he was dead!"

—WARREN HOLL

Altar Egos

The groom and his best man were sitting together at a table, playing poker in a small room at the back of the church. Their jackets were off, their sleeves rolled up and each man was viewing the cards he had been dealt. The door suddenly swung open, and the angry bride came barging in.

"What do you two think you're doing here? The ceremony is about to begin!" screamed the bride.

"Honey," replied the groom, "you know it's bad luck for the groom to see the bride before the wedding!"

—ROBERT HALSTEAD

At an Italian wedding ceremony, the priest asked the bride, "Do you take Franco Giuseppe Antonio to be your husband?"

Looking confused, she said, "Father, there's a mistake. I'm only marrying Frank."

—L. C.

How lovely you look, my dear!" gushed a wedding guest to the bride. And then she whispered, "Whatever happened to that dizzy blonde your groom used to date?"

"I dyed my hair," replied the bride.

—KEVIN BENNINGFIELD in Louisville, Ky., *Courier-Journal*

A Cockney asked a Roman Catholic coworker's help in choosing a bride. "I'm torn between Betty and Maria," he said. "'Ow do you Catholics make decisions?"

"I go to church," said his pal. "Then I look up and pray, and the answer comes to me."

Next day the Cockney was all excited. "I did what you told me, mate, and the answer was given to me!"

"What happened?"

"I went to your church, knelt in prayer, looked up and there it was! Written in gold, 'igh above a stained-glass window."

"What did it say?"

"It said, 'ave Maria."

—*The Jokesmith*

Overheard: "Marriage is nature's way of keeping people from fighting with strangers."

—ALAN KING

Attending a wedding for the first time, a little girl whispered to her mother, "Why is the bride dressed in white?"

"Because white is the color of happiness," her mother explained. "And today is the happiest day of her life."

The child thought about this for a moment. "So why is the groom wearing black?"

—JERRY H. SIMPSON JR.

Why did you marry your husband?" asked the neighborhood gossip. "You don't seem to have much in common."

"It was the old story of opposites attracting each other," explained the wife. "I was pregnant and he wasn't."

—*Parts Pups*

After issuing driver's licenses for 20 years, a clerk was transferred to the marriage license bureau. Almost at once, he was in trouble. Young couples were leaving his desk red-faced and angry. His supervisor asked what was wrong.

"I can't seem to help it," muttered the dismayed clerk. "I just can't get out of the habit of asking whether they want the license for business or for pleasure."

—FRANK SCHAFF

Two neighbors were talking over the back fence. "I went to a wedding this weekend," said one, "but I don't think the marriage will last."

"Why not?" asked the other.

"Well, when the bride said 'I do,' the groom said, 'Don't use that tone of voice with me.' "

—Gary Apple in *Speaker's Idea File*

I had almost made up my mind to attend my friend's wedding when my attention was drawn to the last sentence of the wedding invitation. In bold letters it stated, "Please avoid presence."

—ROBBY ABRAHAM

A man fond of weddings was being married for a fourth time. The groom seemed very moved as he stood at the altar with his new bride, and as he stood dabbing his eyes after the ceremony, his concerned best man asked him why he was so emotional.

"Well," replied the groom, "it just occurred to me that this could be my last wedding."

—BERTE GODERSTAD

For Better or Perverse

A husband and wife drove for miles in silence after a terrible argument in which neither would budge. The husband pointed to a mule in a pasture.

"Relative of yours?" he asked.

"Yes," she replied. "By marriage."

—Bobbie Mae Cooley in *The American Legion Magazine*

Executive overheard talking to a friend: "My wife tells me I don't display enough passion. Imagine! I have a good mind to send her a memo."

—*Speaker's Idea File*

Let's get one thing straight," the newlywed said to her husband. "I'm not cleaning up after you. I'm a career woman. That means I pay other people to do housework. Got it?"

"How much?"

"Eight dollars an hour. Take it or leave it."

—Bill Holbrook, King Features Syndicate

Did you hear about the dentist who married a manicurist? They fought tooth and nail.

—Joan McCourt

John, an avant-garde painter, got married. Someone asked the bride a few weeks after the wedding, "How's married life, Helen?"

"It's great," she answered. "My husband paints, I cook; then we try to guess what he painted and what I cooked."

—Mrs. Istvan Pap

• •

Three Frenchmen were trying to define *savoir-faire*. "If I go home," said Alphonse, "and find my wife with another man, say 'Excuse me' and leave, that is savoir-faire."

"No," replied Pierre, "if I go home and find my wife with another man, and say 'Excuse me, please continue,' that is savoir-faire."

"*Au contraire*," said Jacques, "if I go home and find my wife with another man and say 'Excuse me, please continue,' and he can continue, then he has savoir-faire."

—Quoted by Susie Teltser-Schwarz in
Nite Lights

Arnold complained to a coworker that he didn't know what to get his wife for her birthday. "She already has everything you could think of, and anyway, she can buy herself whatever she likes."

"Here's an idea," said the coworker. "Make up your own gift certificate that says, 'Thirty minutes of great loving, any way you want it.' I guarantee she'll be enchanted."

The next day, Arnold's coworker asked, "Well? Did you take my suggestion?"

"Yes," said Arnold.

"Did she like it?"

"Oh, yes! She jumped up, kissed me on the forehead, and ran out the door yelling, 'See you in 30 minutes!' "

—Tom Matthews

Kevin: "My wife and I argue a lot. She's very touchy—the least little thing sets her off."

Christopher: "You're lucky. Mine is a self-starter."

—Ron Dentinger in the
Dodgeville, Wis., *Chronicle*

"Look, I know its not perfect, but, by and large, the jury system has worked very well for our marriage."

The judge was trying to change the mind of a woman filing for divorce. "You're 92," he said. "Your husband's 94. You've been married for 73 years. Why give up now?"

"Our marriage has been on the rocks for quite a while," the woman explained, "but we decided to wait until the children died."

—Quoted by JOYCE BROTHERS

John, I can see that all your buttons are sewed on perfectly. You must be married!"

"That's right. Sewing on buttons was the first thing my wife taught me on our honeymoon."

—*Chayan*

A doctor and his wife were having a big argument at breakfast. "You aren't so good in bed either!" he shouted and stormed off to work. By midmorning, he decided he'd better make amends and phoned home. After many rings, his wife picked up the phone.

"What took you so long to answer?"

"I was in bed."

"What were you doing in bed this late?"

"Getting a second opinion."

—EDWARD B. WORBY

I was relaxing in my favorite chair on Sunday," said one office worker to another, "reading the newspaper, watching a ball game on TV and listening to another on the radio, drinking beer, eating a snack, and scratching the dog with my foot—and my wife has the nerve to accuse me of just sitting there doing nothing!"

—LOLA BRANDLI

Congratulating a friend after her son and daughter got married within a month of each other, a woman asked, "What kind of boy did your daughter marry?"

"Oh, he's wonderful," gushed the mother. "He lets her sleep late, wants her to go to the beauty parlor regularly, and insists on taking her out to dinner every night."

"That's nice," said the woman. "What about your son?"

"I'm not so happy about that," the mother sighed. "His wife sleeps late, spends all her time in the beauty parlor, and makes them eat take-out meals!"

—SABEEN

First man: I can't think what to get my wife for Christmas. If I give her something practical, I know she'll burst into tears.

Second man: In that case, buy her some handkerchiefs.

—MUSTAFA AMMI

The guys down at the bowling alley figure the delivery man has seduced every woman on our street except one," Harvey told his wife.

She thought for a moment. "I'll bet it's that snooty Mrs. Jenkins."

—G. L. GAUKROGER

Over breakfast one morning, a woman said to her husband, "I bet you don't know what day this is."

"Of course I do," he indignantly answered, going out the door on his way to the office.

At 10 AM, the doorbell rang, and when the woman opened the door, she was handed a box containing a dozen long-stemmed red roses. At 1 PM, a foil-wrapped, two-pound box of her favorite chocolates arrived. Later, a boutique delivered a designer dress.

The woman couldn't wait for her husband to come home. "First the flowers, then the candy, and then the dress!" she exclaimed. "I've never spent a more wonderful Groundhog Day in my whole life!"

—EVA C. BEAN

I was talking with an elderly relative who had just celebrated his 55th wedding anniversary. "Are there any secrets between you two?" I asked. "Do you ever hide anything from each other?"

"Well, yes," replied the old man with a sly smile. "I have ten thousand dollars in a bank that Mary doesn't know about. And she has ten thousand in a bank that I don't know about."

—JAMES A. SANAKER

A couple walking in the park noticed a young man and woman sitting on a bench, passionately kissing.

"Why don't you do that?" said the wife.

"Honey," replied her husband, "I don't even know that woman!"

—GARY R. HANDLEY

•••

A man had just presented his wife with the fox coat she had been coaxing and cajoling him to buy her for weeks. Now he was perplexed to see her examining it with a sad look.

"What's the matter, sweetheart? Don't you like the coat?" he asked.

"I love it," she answered. "It's just that I was feeling sorry for the poor little creature who was skinned alive so that I could have the pleasure of wearing this coat."

"Why, thank you," said the husband.

—AMAL KHALIDI

I've finally found a way to get money out of my husband," a woman told her friend. "We were arguing last night, and I told him I was going home to Mother. He gave me the fare."

—CHARLES DONNE

Why Some Species Eat Their Young

A man was walking along a street when from the other side of a wall he heard someone shout, "Fifty-two!"

He stopped, and again he heard, "Fifty-two!"

Unable to overcome his curiosity, the man stood on a box that he found at the spot, peeked over, and a boy hit him with a handful of clay and shouted, "Fifty-three!"

—JULIO CESAR DA CRUZ

Wife: "Donald, when was the last time we received a letter from our son?"

Husband: "Just a second, honey, I'll go look in the checkbook."

—*Die Weltwoche*

"Wait a minute! I smell toys."

Edgar, father of nine, reflected on how he had mellowed over the years: "When the firstborn coughed or sneezed, I called the ambulance. When the last one swallowed a dime, I just told him it was coming out of his allowance."

—JEAN SHORT

My mother always told me I wouldn't amount to anything because I procrastinate," says comedian Judy Tenuta. "I told her, 'Just wait.'"

•••

Mummy has no idea how to raise children," said the child to his father.

"How can you say such a thing?" replied the father.

"Well, Mummy always sends me to bed at night when I'm not sleepy, and wakes me up in the morning when I am."

—Sandor Szabo

The young wife found her husband at their baby's crib, a mixture of emotions spreading over his face. She slipped her arms around him. "A penny for your thoughts," she said, her eyes glistening.

"For the life of me," he replied, "I can't see how anybody can make a crib like this for $84.97."

—H. B. McClung

A little girl asked her mother for ten cents to give to an old lady in the park. Her mother was touched by the child's kindness and gave her the required sum.

"There you are, my dear," said the mother. "But, tell me, isn't the lady able to work any more?"

"Oh yes," came the reply. "She sells sweets."

—Harillon and Suzanne LeClercq

A couple, desperate to conceive a child, went to their priest and asked him to pray for them. "I'm going on a sabbatical to Rome," he replied, "and while I'm there, I'll light a candle for you."

When the priest returned three years later, he went to the couple's house and found the wife pregnant, busily attending to two sets of twins. Elated, the priest asked her where her husband was so that he could congratulate him.

"He's gone to Rome," came the harried reply, "to blow that candle out."

—Elizabeth Benoit

Betsy: "If you have $2, and you ask your father for $4, how much will you have?"

Billy: "Two dollars."

Betsy: "You don't know your math."

Billy: "You don't know my father."

—LISA MCNEASE

My Mary is so smart, she walked when she was eight months old," bragged one woman.

"You call that intelligent?" challenged her companion. "When my Cindy was that old, she let us carry her."

—ARD-JAN DANNENBERG

A girl watched, fascinated, as her mother smoothed cold cream on her face. "Why do you do that?" she asked.

"To make myself beautiful," said the mother, who began removing the cream with a tissue.

"What's the matter?" asked the girl. "Giving up?"

—NANCY C. BELL

Seven-year-old John had finished his summer vacation and gone back to school. Two days later his teacher phoned his mother to tell her that John was misbehaving.

"Wait a minute," she said. "I had John here for two months and I never called you once when he misbehaved."

—F. TRACEY

But, dear," said the mother to her little kid, "I didn't hear you cry when you cut your finger!"

"What's the use of crying? I thought you were outside the house."

—HANI RUSHDI GHEBRI BESHAY

Mrs. Smith was preparing dinner when little Brad came into the kitchen. "What has mama's darling been doing all day?"

"I've been playing mailman," replied Brad.

"Mailman?" asked the mother. "How could you do that when you had no letters?"

"I had a whole bunch of letters," said Brad. "I found them in that old trunk up in the attic, all tied up with ribbon. I put one in every mailbox on the street."

—H. B. McClung

I was a very unpopular child," says comedian Rita Rudner. "I had only two friends. They were imaginary. And they would only play with each other."

The Rogue's Calorie

Horace grabbed his plate and walked up to the party buffet for the fourth time. "Aren't you embarrassed to go back for so many helpings?" asked his wife.

"Not a bit," Horace replied. "I keep telling them it's for you."

—Elinor Filice in *Woman's World*

Heard about the new diet? You eat whatever you want whenever you want, and as much as you want. You don't lose any weight, but it's really easy to stick to.

—George J. Tricker

Comic J. Scott Homan said he'd been trying to get in shape doing 20 sit-ups each morning. "That may not sound like a lot, but you can only hit that snooze alarm so many times."

—Atlanta *Journal-Constitution*

Don't tell me to reduce, Doc," said the man after his examination. "I just can't take those diets."

"No problem," said the doctor. "I'm prescribing an exercise machine."

"Really? What kind?"

"A rack. For your weight, you should be a foot and a half taller."

—GENE NEWMAN

Darn!" the man said to his pal while weighing himself in a drugstore. "I began this diet yesterday, but the scale says I'm *heavier.* Here, Norm, hold my jacket. . . . It *still* says I'm heavier. Here, hold my Twinkies."

—KEVIN FAGAN,
United Features Syndicate

How do you account for your longevity?" asked the reporter on Harvey's 110th birthday.

"You might call me a health nut," Harvey replied. "I never smoked. I never drank. I was always in bed and sound asleep by 10 o'clock. And I've always walked three miles a day, rain or shine."

"But," said the reporter, "I had an uncle who followed that exact routine and died when he was 62. How come it didn't work for him?"

"All I can say," replied Harvey, "is that he didn't keep it up long enough."

—Quoted in *Lutheran Digest*

Q: How do you get a man to do sit-ups?
A: Put the remote control between his feet.

—KATIE KENDRICK

"That weight I lost . . . I found it!"

Are the slimming exercises doing you any good?" a man asked his beer-bellied colleague. "Can you touch your toes now?"

"No, I can't touch them," the other replied, "but I'm beginning to see them."

—Fritz Heidi

The doctor told Uncle Fudd that if he ran five miles a day for 300 days, he would lose 75 pounds. At the end of 300 days, Uncle Fudd called the doctor to report he had lost the weight, but he had a problem.

"What's the problem?" asked the doctor.

"I'm 1,500 miles from home."

—H. B. McClung

I never eat food with additives or preservatives," boasted a health fanatic. "And I never touch anything that's been sprayed or fed chemical grain."

"Wow, that's wonderful," her friend marveled. "How do you feel?"

"Hungry," she moaned.

—S. Bader in *Woman's World*

Did you hear about the man who was arrested for paying his check at a cafeteria with a counterfeit 10-dollar bill?

He had been served decaffeinated coffee with a nondairy creamer and an artificial sweetener.

—Aldo Cammarota

There's a new garlic diet around. You don't lose weight, but you look thinner from a distance.

—Red Shea on *The Tommy Hunter Show*, TNN, Nashville

Those three hams you sold me last month were delicious," the woman told her butcher.

"If you want more, I still have 10 of the same quality."

"Give me your word they're from the same pig, and I'll take three of them."

—*Almanaque Bertrand*

●●●

When short hemlines came back into fashion, a woman dug an old miniskirt out of her closet. She tried it on, but couldn't figure out what to do with the other leg.

—ASHLEY COOPER in the Charleston, S.C.,
News and Courier

Man to clerk in video store: "I'd like to exchange this diet-and-workout tape for one on self-acceptance."

—KEVIN FAGAN,
United Features Syndicate

We're Only Human

George Burns punctuated this story with a flick of his cigar. "A woman said to me, 'Is it true that you still go out with young girls?' I said yes, it's true. She said, 'Is it true that you still smoke 15 to 20 cigars a day?' I said yes, it's true. She said, 'Is it true that you still take a few drinks every day?' I said yes, it's true.

"She said, 'What does your doctor say?' I said, 'He's dead.' "

In New York City," notes comedian Jay Leno, "they're handing out condoms to high-school students. Gee, I thought it was a big day when I got my class ring!"

At a party several young couples were discussing the difficulties of family budgets. "I really don't want a lot of money," said one yuppie. "I just wish we could afford to live the way we're living now."

—*The Lion*

My parents are the epitome of abstinence," the boy explains to his schoolmates.

"They don't smoke, they don't drink, and my sister and I are adopted children."

—*Weltwoche*

Two men were sitting by the swimming pool at a nudist colony when they noticed a beautiful young woman walking toward the pool. Her tan lines traced the outline of a tiny bathing suit with elaborately crisscrossed straps across the back.

"Mmm," one of the men said wistfully, "I'll bet she looks great in that suit."

—BARBARA HADLEY, quoted by Patricia McLaughlin in the Philadelphia *Inquirer Magazine*

A 90-year-old man checked into a posh hotel to celebrate his birthday. As a surprise, some friends sent a call girl to his room. When the man answered his door, he saw before him a beautiful young woman. "I have a present for you," she said.

"Really?" replied the bewildered gent.

"I'm here to give you super sex," she said in a whisper.

"Thanks," he said thoughtfully. "I'll take the soup."

—DORIAN GOLDSTEIN

Two friends are talking about their reading:

"I'm fascinated by medical publications. A friend of mine treated herself, using articles she read in the journals."

"You're speaking of her in the past tense. Did she die?"

"Unfortunately."

"Of what?"

"A typographical error."

—MAURICE OOGHE

Q: What's the definition of a bachelor pad?

A: All the house plants are dead, but there's something growing in the refrigerator.

—MARSHALL WILLIAMS in *The Los Angeles Times*

A woman sat down on a park bench, glanced around and decided to stretch out her legs on the seat and relax. After a while, a beggar came up to her and said, "Hello, luv, how's about us going for a walk together?"

"How dare you," retorted the woman, "I'm not one of your cheap pickups!"

"Well then," said the tramp, "what are you doing in my bed?"

—ALZIRA INFANTE DE LA CERDA

To gain self-confidence, you must avoid using negative words such as *can't* and *not*," the counselor advised the young woman. "Do you think you could do that?"

"Well, I can't see why not."

—GREG EVANS, North American Syndicate

Overheard: "I'm trying to keep up with the Joneses, but every time I catch up, they just refinance!"

—DAVID A. SNELL

The best thing about getting older is that you gain sincerity," says Tommy Smothers. "Once you learn to fake that, there's nothing you can't do."

Did you hear about the self-help group for compulsive talkers? It's called On & On Anon.

—SALLY DAVIS

Bill: "Why the glum look?"
Stan: "I just don't understand today's world. My son wears an earring. My daughter has a tattoo. My wife makes twice what I do."
Bill: "So what are you going to do?"
Stan: "I'm thinking of going home to my father."

—*American Speaker*

Heard at a bus stop:
"Hello, Lily, how are you? What have you done to your hair? It looks like a wig."
"Yes, it is a wig."
"Really, how wonderful! It looks just like real hair."

—GANESH V.

One woman was talking to another on the telephone:
"I ran into an old friend from high school the other day and she looked marvelous! She hadn't gained an ounce, and she didn't have a single wrinkle—so I ran into her again."

—*Shoebox Greetings*

"Dear, did something happen at the office?"

The Professions

Open Wide and Say Ha!

Three doctors were on their way to a convention when their car had a flat. They got out and examined the tire. The first doctor said, "I think it's flat."

The second doctor examined it closely and said, "It sure looks flat."

The third doctor felt the tire and said, "It feels like it's flat."

All three nodded their heads in agreement. "We'd better run some tests."

—DENISE BRIGHT

A woman and her husband interrupted their vacation to go to a dentist. "I want a tooth pulled, and I don't want Novocain because I'm in a big hurry," the woman said. "Just extract the tooth as quickly as possible, and we'll be on our way."

The dentist was quite impressed. "You're certainly a courageous woman," he said. "Which tooth is it?"

The woman turned to her husband and said, "Show him your tooth, dear."

—*Portals of Prayer*

Patient: "This hospital is no good. They treat us like dogs."
Orderly: "Mr. Jones, you know that's not true. Now, roll over."

—ANNE WOLOSYN

A physician went to heaven and met God, who granted him one question. So the physician asked, "Will health-care reform ever occur?"

"I have good news and bad news," God replied. "The answer is yes, but not in my lifetime."

—STEPHEN HUBER, MD, in *Medical World News*

A patient was anxious after a prolonged bedside discussion by hospital doctors. The head doctor even came to see him.

"There must be a lot of doubt about what is wrong with me," the patient told the doctor.

"Where did you get that idea?" the doctor replied.

"All the other doctors disagreed with you, didn't they?"

"To some extent, but don't worry," said the doctor consolingly. "In a similar case, I stood firm on my diagnosis—and the post-mortem proved me right!"

—ABBAS ALI ZAHID

A woman accompanied her husband when he went for his annual checkup. While the patient was getting dressed, the doctor came out and said to the wife, "I don't like the way he looks."

"Neither do I," she said. "But he's handy around the house."

—MERRITT K. FREEMAN in *Y. B. News*

A jungle witch doctor was called to treat a man with a high fever. He made a medicine with the eye of a toad, the liver of a snake, the heart of a rat, six black beetles and half a cockroach, all mixed together with slime from the local river.

The next day he went to see his patient and found him no better. "Oh dear," said the witch doctor. "Maybe you had better try a couple of aspirins."

—CHARISMA B. RAMOS

A guy spots his doctor in the mall. He stops him and says, "Six weeks ago when I was in your office, you told me to go home, get into bed and stay there until you called. But you never called."

"I didn't?" the doctor says. "Then what are you doing out of bed?"

—RON DENTINGER in the Dodgeville, Wis., *Chronicle*

"The dentist will see you in a moment."

After giving a woman a full medical examination, the doctor explained his prescription as he wrote it out. "Take the green pill with a glass of water when you get up. Take the blue pill with a glass of water after lunch. Then just before going to bed, take the red pill with another glass of water."

"Exactly what is my problem, Doctor?" the woman asked.

"You're not drinking enough water."

—*Quote*

Doctor," the man said to his ophthalmologist, "I was looking in the mirror this morning, and I noticed that one of my eyes is different from the other!"

"Oh?" replied the doctor. "Which one?"

—JERRY H. SIMPSON JR.

A man called his doctor's office for an appointment. "I'm sorry," said the receptionist, "we can't fit you in for at least two weeks."

"But I could be dead by then!"

"No problem. If your wife lets us know, we'll cancel the appointment."

—RON DENTINGER in the Dodgeville, Wis., *Chronicle*

The woman went to a dentist to have her false teeth adjusted for the fifth time. She said they still didn't fit. "Well," said the dentist, "I'll do it again this time, but no more. There's no reason why these shouldn't fit your mouth easily."

"Who said anything about my mouth?" the woman answered. "They don't fit in the glass!"

—*The Speaker's Handbook of Humor,*
edited by Maxwell Droke

The hospital patient was worried. "Are you sure it's pneumonia, Doctor?" he asked. "I've heard of cases where a doctor treated a patient for pneumonia, and he ended up dying of something else."

"Don't worry," said the doctor. "When I treat a patient for pneumonia, he dies of pneumonia."

—WINSTON K. PENDLETON,
Funny Stories, Jokes and Anecdotes

It's the Law!

The law professor was lecturing on courtroom procedure.

"When you are fighting a case and have the facts on your side, hammer away at the facts. If you have the law on your side, hammer away with the law."

"But what if you have neither the facts nor the law on your side?"

"In that case," said the professor, "hammer away on the table."

—The Rotarian

What possible excuse can you give for acquitting this defendant?" the judge shouted at the jury.

"Insanity, Your Honor," replied the foreman.

"All 12 of you?"

—MARTHA J. BECKMAN in *Modern Maturity*

You admit having broken into the dress shop four times?" asked the judge.

"Yes," answered the suspect.

"And what did you steal?"

"A dress, Your Honor," replied the suspect.

"One dress?" echoed the judge. "But you admit breaking in four times!"

"Yes, Your Honor," sighed the suspect. "But three times my wife didn't like the color."

—The Jewish Press

And did you hear about the lawyer who didn't like what the restaurant offered? He asked for a change of menu.

—BILL NELSON in the
Milwaukee *Journal*

"It's a deal, but just to be on the safe side let's have our lawyers look at this handshake."

A young executive stomped into the elevator, obviously upset. "What's the matter?" asked a businessman standing there.

"Nepotism!" shouted the first man. "My boss just bypassed me and made his nephew office manager!"

"I see," the other said, handing over his business card. "If you need legal advice, please call me."

The young man glanced at the card: "O'Brien, O'Brien, O'Brien and O'Brien, Attorneys at Law."

—NORMAN F. PIHALY

The lawyer was cross-examining a witness. "Isn't it true," he bellowed, "that you were given $500 to throw this case?"

The witness did not answer. Instead, he just stared out the window as though he hadn't heard the question. The attorney repeated himself, again getting the same reaction—no response.

Finally, the judge spoke to the witness, "Please answer the question."

"Oh," said the startled witness, "I thought he was talking to you."

—*Sunshine* Magazine

A man visiting a graveyard saw a tombstone that read: "Here lies John Kelly, a lawyer and an honest man."

"How about that!" he exclaimed. "They've got three people buried in one grave."

—LOUISE MAYER in *Capper's*

Your Honor," began the defense attorney, "my client has been characterized as an incorrigible bank robber, without a single socially redeeming feature. I intend to disprove that."

"And how will you accomplish this?" the judge inquired.

"By proving beyond a shadow of a doubt," replied the lawyer, "that the note my client handed the teller was on recycled paper."

—R. C. SHEBELSKI

Before a burglary trial, the judge explained to the defendant, "You can let me try your case, or you can choose to have a jury of your peers."

The man thought for a moment. "What are peers?" he asked.

"They're people just like you—your equals."

"Forget it," retorted the defendant. "I don't want to be tried by a bunch of thieves."

—JOEY ADAMS

*"Your Honor, the relevance of this line of questioning
will become apparent in a moment."*

THE PROFESSIONS

I'll need to see your license and registration," says the highway patrolman after stopping a middle-aged couple. "You were speeding."

"But, officer," says the husband, "I was way under the speed limit."

"Sir, you were doing 63 in a 55 zone."

"I was not speeding!" insists the man. "Your radar gun must be broken."

At this point, the wife leans over. "It's no use arguing with him, officer," she says apologetically. "He always gets this stubborn when he's been drinking."

—LISA MALLETTE

In darkest night, a policeman watches a staggering man trying in vain to unlock a door.

"Is this your home, after all?" the policeman asks.

"Sure, I'll prove it to you if you help me."

Inside, the man explains, "You see, this is my bedroom. And this is my wife."

"And who is the man next to her?" the policeman wants to know.

"That's me!"

—RENÉ GUYER

A junior partner in a law firm called his staff in for a meeting. "I have good news and bad news," he said, grinning. "Which do you want first?" The staff groaned, and agreed they'd better get the bad news first. "Okay," said the junior partner, "we are going to downsize. Half of you won't be here tomorrow. And the others may stay at a substantial reduction in salary."

The staff stood in horrified shock. Finally, one asked in a trembling voice, "What's the good news?"

The boss beamed. "I've been made a *full* partner!"

—*The Jokesmith*

Shrink Rap

Hello, welcome to the Psychiatric Hotline.

"If you are obsessive-compulsive, please press 1 repeatedly.

"If you are co-dependent, please ask someone to press 2.

"If you have multiple personalities, please press 3, 4, 5 and 6.

"If you are paranoid-delusional, we know who you are and what you want. Just stay on the line until we can trace the call.

"If you are schizophrenic, listen carefully and a little voice will tell you which number to press.

"If you are manic-depressive, it doesn't matter which number you press. No one will answer."

—JACQUELYN MAYERHOFER

The psychiatrist was interviewing a first-time patient. "You say you're here," he inquired, "because your family is worried about your taste in socks?"

"That's correct," muttered the patient. "I like wool socks."

"But that's perfectly normal," replied the doctor. "Many people prefer wool socks to those made from cotton or acrylic. In fact, I myself like wool socks."

"You DO?" exclaimed the man. "With oil and vinegar or just a squeeze of lemon?"

—PHYLLIS THATCHER

Psychiatrist: "Why can't you sleep at night?"

Patient: "Because I'm trying to solve all the world's problems."

Psychiatrist: "Ever get them solved?"

Patient: "Almost every time."

Psychiatrist: "Then why can't you sleep?"

Patient: "The ticker-tape parades they hold for me keep me awake."

—*Funny, Funny World*

"Get me a psychiatrist, preferably one with military experience."

Psychiatrist to patient: "You have nothing to worry about—anyone who can pay my bills is certainly not a failure."

—LEA BERNER

Q: Why is psychoanalysis a lot quicker for men than for women?
A: When it's time to go back to their childhood, they're already there.

—MARTHA J. KIELEK

Don't worry," a patient told his psychiatrist. "I'll pay every cent I owe or my name isn't Alexander the Great!"
—*The Return of the Good Clean Jokes*, compiled by Bob Phillips

Is it true that Natalie's son is seeing a psychiatrist?" a woman asked her friend.

"That's what I heard," she answered.

"So what's his problem?"

"The doctor says that what he has is a terrible Oedipus complex."

"Oedipus-schmoedipus—as long as he loves his mother."

—LEO ROSTEN, *Hooray for Yiddish*

Three women started boasting about their sons. "What a birthday I had last year!" exclaimed the first. "My son, that wonderful boy, threw me a big party in a fancy restaurant. He even paid for plane tickets for my friends."

"That's very nice, but listen to this," said the second. "Last winter, my son gave me an all-expenses-paid cruise to the Greek islands. First class."

"That's nothing!" interrupted the third. "For five years now, my son has been paying a psychiatrist $150 an hour, three times a week. And the whole time he talks about nothing but me."

—*Current Comedy*

An unhappy man told his friend that he was seeing a psychiatrist about his marital problems. The shrink told him that his wife probably didn't mean the cruel things she was saying about him.

"My doctor said I have a persecution complex," the patient told his friend.

"Really? And what do you think?" the friend asked.

"That's what I expected he'd say," the man replied. "The guy hates me."

—RON DENTINGER in the Dodgeville, Wis., *Chronicle*

Jackson went to a psychiatrist. "Doc," he said, "I've got trouble. Every time I get into bed I think there's somebody under it. I get under the bed, I think there's somebody on top of it. Top, under, top, under. I'm goin' crazy!"

"Just put yourself in my hands for two years," said the shrink. "Come to me three times a week, and I'll cure you."

"How much do you charge?"

"A hundred dollars per visit."

"I'll think about it."

Jackson never went back. Six months later he met the doctor on the street. "Why didn't you ever come to see me again?" asked the psychiatrist.

"For a hundred bucks a visit? A bartender cured me for 10 dollars."

"Is that so! How?"

"He told me to cut the legs off the bed."

—LARRY WILDE, *The Ultimate Jewish Joke Book*

John, having completed a course of analysis with his psychiatrist, to friend: "I always thought I was indecisive."

Friend: "And now?"

John: "I'm not so sure."

—MRS. P. J. WOOD

Tricks of the Trades

An inexperienced real-estate salesman asked his boss if he could refund the deposit to an angry customer who had discovered that the lot he had bought was under water.

"What kind of salesman are you?" the boss scolded. "Get out there and sell him a boat."

—Felix Tesarski

The reading material at the barber shop consisted entirely of murder stories, mysteries, thrillers, and ghost tales.

When I asked the barber if he wanted to terrify his customers he replied, "No sir. These books make the customers' hair stand up and then it becomes easier to trim and cut."

—N. Ravi

After being laid off from five different jobs in four months, Arnold was hired by a warehouse. But one day he lost control of a forklift and drove it off the loading dock. Surveying the damage, the owner shook his head and said he'd have to withhold 10 percent of Arnold's wages to pay for the repairs. "How much will it cost?" asked Arnold.

"About $4,500," said the owner.

"What a relief!" exclaimed Arnold. "I've finally got job security!"

—DAVID E. SEES

Pete was telling a friend that he had just lost his job. "Why did the foreman fire you?" the friend asked in surprise.

"Oh," Pete said, "you know how foremen are. They stand around with their hands in their pockets watching everybody else work."

"We all know that," replied his friend. "But why did he let you go?"

"Jealousy," answered Pete. "All the other workers thought I was the foreman."

—*Sunshine* Magazine

A professor of English and the editor of the local newspaper had many friendly arguments. One Friday evening the professor was walking out of a local club with a bottle of whiskey wrapped in that day's newspaper.

"Oh!" said the editor, who was walking past. "Looks like there's something interesting in that paper."

"Aye," replied the professor. "It's the most interesting item that's been in it all week."

—ARTHUR FULLER

H ow's your new job at the factory?" one guy asked another.

"I'm not going back there."

"Why not?"

"For many reasons," he answered. "The sloppiness, the shoddy workmanship, the awful language—they just couldn't put up with it."

—MELL LAZARUS,
Creators Syndicate

A businessman was dining at a fancy restaurant and, so the story goes, met Lee Iacocca by the phone booth. "Mr. Iacocca," he gushed, "*the* American business hero! I've studied your career, and any success I've had comes from emulating you. Would you do me a favor? I'm with some colleagues. Please come by my table, say 'Hello, Harry,' and let me introduce you. It would mean so much to me."

Iacocca agreed. He waited for the man to sit down and then walked toward his table.

"Holy smoke!" cried one of Harry's friends. "It's Lee Iacocca, and he's heading this way!"

"Hello, Harry!" Iacocca said. "Introduce me to your friends."

Harry looked at him blankly. "Come back later, Lee," he said. "We're trying to have lunch."

—*The Jokesmith*

A pproaching a passer-by, a street person asked, "Sir, would you give me a hundred dollars for a cup of coffee?"

"That's ridiculous!" the man replied.

"Just a yes or no, fella," the beggar growled. "I don't need a lecture about how to run my business."

—*Playboy*

I hear the boys are gonna strike," one worker told another.

"What for?" asked the friend.

"Shorter hours."

"Good for them. I always did think 60 minutes was too long for an hour."

—Tal D. Bonham, *The Treasury of Clean Country Jokes*

Bill attended a party where he met an old acquaintance. "Hello, Sam," he said. "How's your clothing business? I heard you lost a lot on that fall shipment of dresses."

"That's right," Sam responded.

"And you almost went bankrupt."

"That's true too."

"But I understand you made a big profit on another shipment and wound up having a pretty good season after all."

"That's correct. Then I guess you heard all about it, Bill."

"Yeah," Bill answered, "but this is the first time I'm hearing all the details."

—*Myron Cohen's Big Joke Book*

Three businessmen were having dinner at a club. When it came time to pay the check, each grabbed for it.

"It's a business expense," said one.

"I'll pay," said the second. "I'm on cost plus."

"Let me have it," argued the third. "I'm filing for bankruptcy next week."

—Joey Adams

"I've stopped going out at night. Too dangerous."

Ned took a job working alone in Canada's far frozen north. "Here's your emergency survival kit," said his boss. "It contains a box of flares, a radio, and a deck of cards."

"What are the cards for?" Ned asked.

"In case the flares don't work and the radio freezes up," replied the boss, "just take out the cards and play solitaire. In about 10 seconds someone will tap you on the shoulder and say, 'Put the red 9 on the black 10.'"

—KEVIN HILGERS in *One to One*

Football player's wife: "I hate it when my husband calls leftovers 'replays.'"

TV executive's wife: "My husband calls them 'reruns.'"

Mortician's wife: "Be grateful. My husband refers to them as 'remains.'"

—LESLIE BARANOWSKY

A very successful businessman had a meeting with his new son-in-law. "I love my daughter, and now I welcome you into the family," said the man. "To show you how much we care for you, I'm making you a 50-50 partner in my business. All you have to do is go to the factory every day and learn the operation."

The son-in-law interrupted. "I hate factories. I can't stand the noise."

"I see," replied the father-in-law. "Well, then you'll work in the office and take charge of some of the operations."

"I hate office work," said the son-in-law. "I can't stand being stuck behind a desk."

"Wait a minute," said the father-in-law. "I just made you half-owner of a money-making organization, but you don't like factories and won't work in an office. What am I going to do with you?"

"Easy," said the young man. "Buy me out."

—*Gene Perrett's Funny Business*

The Armed Farces

During our basic army training, a sergeant was telling us how a submachine gun sprayed bullets. He drew a circle on a blackboard and announced that it had 260 degrees.

"But, sergeant, all circles have 360 degrees," someone called out.

"Don't be stupid," the sergeant roared. "This is a small circle."

—C. A. Sutton

A tail gunner was being court-martialed. "What did you hear in your headset?" demanded a superior officer.

"Well," replied the airman, "I heard my squadron leader holler, 'Enemy planes at 5 o'clock!' "

"What action did you take?" persisted another officer.

"Why, sir," replied the gunner, "I just sat back and waited. It was only 4:30."

—Jerry Lieberman, *3,500 Good Jokes for Speakers*

During a training exercise, an army unit was late for afternoon inspection. "Where are those camouflage trucks?" the irate colonel barked.

"They're here somewhere," replied the sergeant, "but we can't find 'em."

—L. Downing

What's the matter with you, lad?"

"Typhoid fever, Sergeant."

"That illness either kills you or leaves you an idiot. I know because I've had it!"

—Ana Maria Santos

Through the pitch-black night, the captain sees a light dead ahead on a collision course with his ship. He sends a signal: "Change your course 10 degrees east."

The light signals back: "Change yours, 10 degrees west."

Angry, the captain sends: "I'm a navy captain! Change your course, sir!"

"I'm a seaman, second class," comes the reply. "Change your course, sir."

Now the captain is furious. "I'm a battleship! I'm not changing course!"

There's one last reply. "I'm a lighthouse. Your call."

—Dan Bell

A sergeant put this problem to a recruit: "Suppose it's wartime. You're walking in the woods, and you suddenly come up against 10 of the enemy. What would you do?"

After a moment's silence the recruit's face brightened, and he replied, "Surround them, Sergeant."

—E. Meutstege

While conducting a routine inspection, the colonel arrived at the mess hall door where he met two KPs with a large soup kettle.

"Let me taste that," the colonel snapped.

One of the men fetched a big spoon and handed it respectfully to the CO, who plunged the ladle into the pot and took a large mouthful of the steaming liquid, smacking his lips critically.

Then he let out a roar that could be heard back at headquarters. "Do you call that soup?" he bellowed.

"No, sir," explained one of the KPs. "It's dishwater we were just throwing out."

—James Mutch

Top brass from the Army, Navy, and Marine Corps were arguing about who had the bravest troops. They decided to settle the dispute using an enlisted man from each branch.

The army general called a private over and ordered him to climb to the top of the base flagpole while singing "The Caissons Go Rolling Along," then let go with both hands, and salute. The private quickly complied.

Next, the admiral ordered a sailor to climb the pole, polish the brass knob at the top, sing "Anchors Aweigh," salute smartly, and jump off. The sailor did as he was told and landed on the concrete below.

Finally the marine was told to do exactly as the army and navy men had done, but in full battle gear, pack filled with bricks, loaded weapon carried high. He took one look at the marine general and said, "You're out of your mind, sir!"

The marine commander turned to the others. "Now *that's* guts!"

—RICHARD BECTON

One hazard of wartime training in England was that road signs were removed when invasion seemed imminent. A cartoon in an English newspaper during the invasion scare of 1940 pictured two German paratroopers scanning a map at a railway station. Over their heads was the one remaining sign: Gentlemen.

"I can't find this place on the map," says one to the other.

—STROME GALLOWAY in *Legion*

It happened that the platoon leader forgot the expression "Mark time." Without losing his composure, he faced his platoon and shouted, "Ten-shut! Pretend to go but don't; pretend to go but don't; pretend to go but don't . . . ."

—SYLVIA MENDES DE ABREU

"You're lucky. You never have to worry about having a bad clothes day."

During a simulated attack, the troops have to defend themselves against an imaginary enemy, as the sergeant calls it. Bawling out orders, he notices that one recruit shows little response.

"You there," the sergeant shouts, "the imaginary enemy is advancing, and you're caught in the crossfire. Action!"

The recruit takes two steps to one side.

"What are you doing, man?" yells the sergeant, purple with fury.

"I'm taking shelter behind an imaginary tree, Sergeant," answers the recruit calmly.

—MICHEL VAN KERCKHOVEN

Office Antics

One winter morning, an employee explained why he had shown up for work 45 minutes late. "It was so slippery out that for every step I took ahead, I slipped back two."

The boss eyed him suspiciously. "Oh, yeah? Then how did you ever get here?"

"I finally gave up," he said, "and started for home."

—ERIC WIGHT

Say, Bill," a man said to his pal, "how do you like your new job?"

"It's the worst job I ever had."

"How long have you been there?"

"About three months."

"Why don't you quit?"

"No way. This is the first time in 20 years that I've looked forward to going home."

—JIM YOUNG

Employee: "The stress my boss puts me under is killing me. I have migraines, my blood pressure is going through the roof, I can't sleep at night, I just found out I have an ulcer, and as long as I stay in this job, the only question is whether I'll have a stroke or a heart attack."

Friend: "So why don't you quit?"

Employee: "I have a great health plan."

—RICHARD JEROME in *The Sciences*

A lot of people complain about their dumb boss," says Joey Adams. "What they don't realize is that they'd be out of a job if their dumb boss were any smarter."

"Miss Bremmer, get me whatever coast I'm not on."

Dexter had just returned from two weeks of vacation. He asked his boss for two more weeks off to get married.

"What!" shouted the boss. "I can't give you more time now. Why didn't you get married while you were off?"

"Are you nuts?" replied Dexter. "That would have ruined my entire vacation!"

—H. B. McClung

Sign on company bulletin board: "This firm requires no physical-fitness program. Everyone gets enough exercise jumping to conclusions, flying off the handle, running down the boss, flogging dead horses, knifing friends in the back, dodging responsibility, and pushing their luck."

—Financial Times

The stenographer who had worked for nine years in our firm got a job elsewhere and approached the personnel officer for a certificate of experience.

"Make it out for 10 years," the steno suggested.

"But you've worked for only nine years," the personnel officer pointed out.

"But, sir," replied the steno, "what about my overtime?"

—P. R. MOHANAN

One payday, an employee received an unusually large check. She decided not to say anything about it. The following week, her check was for less than the normal amount, and she confronted her boss.

"How come," the supervisor inquired, "you didn't say anything when you were overpaid?"

Unruffled, the employee replied, "Well, I can overlook one mistake—but not two in a row!"

—Farmers Independent

The owner of a big electronics firm called in his personnel director. "My son will be graduating from college soon and needing a job. He's going to be your new assistant, but he's *not* to be shown any favoritism. Treat him just as you would any other son of mine."

—Quoted in *The Rotarian*

Gag-riculture

A cowboy applied for an insurance policy. "Have you ever had any accidents?" asked the agent.

"Nope," said the cowboy, "though a bronc did kick in two of my ribs last year, and a couple of years ago a rattlesnake bit my ankle."

"Wouldn't you call those accidents?" replied the puzzled agent.

"Naw," the cowboy said, "they did it on purpose."

—*Our Daily Bread*

Because of the shortage of jobs in town, a boy appeared for work on a farm. The foreman decided to give him a try and told him to milk a cow, equipping him with a stool and a bucket.

An hour later the boy returned dirty and sweaty, the bucket in one hand and the broken stool in the other.

"Extracting the milk was easy," he explained. "The worst part was getting the cow to sit on the stool!"

—MIGUEL JOSÉ DE OLIVERIA NETO

Willie and Ray, a couple of farmers, met at the town hardware store on Saturday. "Had some problems with my herd," lamented Willie. "My prize bull was impotent. But the vet came and gave him some special medicine, and now he seems to be doing fine."

The next week, Ray met Willie again. "My bull's had problems too," said Ray. "What was that medicine the vet prescribed?"

"I don't know," answered Willie. "But it tastes like chocolate."

—WILLIAM L. HEARTWELL JR.

Van der Merwe was carrying a box when he met his friend. "Guess how many chickens I have in this box and I'll give you both of them," he said.

—*Personality*, Durban

"You want a sign that reads 'The world ends tomorrow' ... when do you have to have it?"

Religion

IN GOOD SPIRITS 68
COLLARED 72
YOU SHOULD DIE LAUGHING 76

In Good Spirits

When Adam came home in the small hours of the morning, Eve was jealous. "But in all of creation," Adam reasoned, "there's no one but you and me." Mollified, Eve snuggled up to him. Still, when he fell asleep, she very carefully counted his ribs.

—BILL SROKA

I used to practice meditation on an old mat. My wife was not happy about the worn-out mat.

One day I found the rug missing from its usual place.

"Where is it?" I asked her sternly.

"It has achieved nirvana," she retorted.

—ANIL BHARTI

A Christian in ancient Rome was being pursued by a lion. He ran through the city streets and into the woods, dodging back and forth among the trees. Finally it became obvious that it was hopeless— the lion was going to catch him. So he turned suddenly, faced the beast and dropped to his knees. "Lord," he prayed desperately, "make this lion a Christian."

Instantly the lion dropped to its knees and prayed, "For this meal of which I am about to partake. . . ."

—VAUNA J. ARMSTRONG

My mother always told me God hears every prayer," says comedian Mary Armstrong. "If I'd pray really hard for something and nothing happened, she would say, 'Sometimes God's answer is no.' But what if God just doesn't answer right away? You could be 42, your needs will have changed, and all of a sudden you look out at your front yard one morning and there's a Shetland pony!"

An impassioned minister was visiting a country church and began his address with a stirring reminder: "Everybody in this parish is going to die."

The evangelist was discomfited to notice a man in the front pew who was smiling broadly. "Why are you so amused?" he asked.

"I'm not in this parish," replied the man. "I'm just visiting my sister for the weekend."

—ROGER DELAHUNTY

Sol strictly observed Jewish dietary laws. But one day he went to a restaurant by himself and noticed roast pig on the menu. *Just once, I'd like to try it,* he thought, and placed his order.

The pig was brought to his table with an apple in its mouth. Just then, Sol looked up, and there was a member of his synagogue staring at him. "So I ordered a baked apple," said Sol innocently. "Who knew how they'd serve it?"

—RUTH SCHWARTZ

A Texan traveled to England on vacation. While there, he attended a religious service and was amazed at how quiet and reserved it was. Not one word was spoken out of turn. All of a sudden he heard the minister say something he really liked. "Amen!" he shouted. Everyone in the church turned and stared, and the usher came running down the aisle.

"You must not talk out loud," admonished the usher.

"But," protested the Texan, "I've got religion!"

"Well," said the usher, "you did not get it here."

—DOROTHY STARLING

Did you hear about the insomniac dyslexic agnostic? He stayed up all night wondering if there really was a dog.

—DANIEL J. KLAIMAN

A preacher was asked to give a talk at a women's health symposium. His wife asked about his topic, but he was too embarrassed to admit that he had been asked to speak about sex. Thinking quickly, he replied, "I'm talking about sailing."

"Oh, that's nice," said his wife.

The next day, at the grocery store, a young woman who had attended the lecture recognized the minister's wife. "That was certainly an excellent talk your husband gave yesterday," she said. "He really has a unique perspective on the subject." Somewhat surprised, the minister's wife replied, "Gee, funny you should think so. I mean, he's only done it twice. The first time he threw up, and the second time, his hat blew off."

—D. E. NORLING

A small town's only barber was known for his arrogant, negative attitude. When one of his customers mentioned he'd be going to Rome on vacation and hoped to meet the pope, the barber's reaction was typical. "You?" he said. "Meet the pope? Don't make me laugh! The pope sees kings and presidents. What would he want with you?"

A month later, the man returned for another haircut. "How was Rome?" asked the barber.

"Great! I saw the pope!"

"From St. Peter's Square, I suppose, with the rest of the crowd," said the barber.

"Yes, but then two guards came up, said the pope wanted to meet me, and took me right into his private apartment in the Vatican."

"Really?" the barber asked. "What did he say?"

"He said, 'Who gave you that lousy haircut?' "

—Quoted in Chelmsford, Mass.,
All Saints Church Newsletter

"My dad says mom is a pagan because she serves
burnt offerings for dinner."

Two fellows, Murphy and Clancy, were walking past the church when Murphy said, "I haven't been to confession for a while. I believe I'll go in and get absolution." Murphy went into the confessional and acknowledged having his way with a lady.

"I know you by your voice, Murphy, and this is not the first time this has happened," said the priest. "I want to know the lady's name."

"It's not proper you should ask, and I'll not be telling you!"

"If you want absolution, you'll be telling me. Was it O'Reilly's sister?" Murphy refused to answer. "I'll ask again. Was it the widow Harrington?" Again, Murphy wouldn't reply. "One more time I'll ask: was it the Flanagan girl?"

"For the third time, I'll not be telling you!" said Murphy.

"Then you'll get no absolution from me. Out with you!"

His friend Clancy was waiting. "Well, did you get absolution?"

"No," said Murphy with a smile. "But I got three good leads!"

—WEBB CASTOR

God: "Whew! I just created a 24-hour period of alternating light and darkness on Earth."

Angel: "What are you going to do now?"

God: "Call it a day."

—DAVE COVERLY, Creators Syndicate

Collared

At a wedding reception, a priest and a rabbi met at the buffet table. "Go ahead," said the priest, "try one of these delicious ham sandwiches. Overlooking your divine rule just this once won't do you any harm."

"That I will do, dear sir," the rabbi replied, "on the day of your wedding!"

—KIM DUBOIS

The newly appointed priest was being briefed by the housekeeper on problems in the rectory that required immediate attention.

"Your roof needs repair, Father," she said. "Your water pressure is bad and your furnace is not working."

"Now, Mrs. Kelly," the priest allowed, "you've been the housekeeper here five years, and I've only been here a few days. Why not say *our* roof and *our* furnace?"

Several weeks later, when the pastor was meeting with the bishop and several other priests, Mrs. Kelly burst into the office terribly upset. "Father, Father," she blurted, "there's a mouse in our room and it's under our bed!"

—DORIS CYPHER

And did you hear about the bishop who hired a secretary who had worked for the Pentagon? She immediately changed his filing system to "Sacred" and "Top Sacred."

—IRA N. BRIGGS

The young couple invited their parson for Sunday dinner. While they were in the kitchen preparing the meal, the minister asked their son what they were having. "Goat," the little boy replied.

"Goat?" replied the startled man of the cloth. "Are you sure about that?"

"Yep," said the youngster. "I heard Pa say to Ma, 'Might as well have the old goat for dinner today as any other day.'"

—PAMELA D. MCMANUS

In a booming voice, a cantor bragged to his congregation, "Two years ago, I insured my voice with Lloyd's of London for $750,000."

The crowded room was hushed. Suddenly, an elderly woman spoke. "So," she said, "what did you do with the money?"

—JOSEPH TELUSHKIN, *Jewish Humor*

"Your sermon helped me understand my soaps better."

A young vicar about to deliver his first sermon asked the advice of a retired minister on how to capture the congregation's attention.

"Start with an opening line that's certain to grab them," the cleric told him. "For example: Some of the best years of my life were spent in the arms of a woman."

He smiled at the young vicar's shocked look before adding, "She was my mother."

The next Sunday the vicar nervously clutched the pulpit rail before the congregation and stated, "Some of the best years of my life were spent in the arms of a woman."

He was pleased at the instant reaction—then panic-stricken. "But for the life of me, I can't remember who she was!"

—GIL HARRIS

A pastor was preaching an impassioned sermon on the evils of television. "It steals away precious time that could be better spent on other things," he said, advising the congregation to do what he and his family had done. "We put our TV away in the closet."

"That's right," his wife mumbled, "and it gets awfully crowded in there."

—SHERRI DORMER

The minister was sick, and a pastor noted for his never-ending sermons agreed to fill in. When he stood up in the pulpit, he was annoyed to find only 10 worshipers present, including the choir. Afterward he complained to the sexton. "That was a very small turnout," he said. "Weren't they informed that I was coming?"

"No," replied the sexton, "but word must have leaked out!"

—Sunday Post

The minister selected a 50-cent item at a convenience store but then discovered he didn't have any money with him.

"I could invite you to hear me preach in return," he said jokingly to the clerk, "but I'm afraid I don't have any 50-cent sermons."

"Perhaps," suggested the clerk, "I could come twice."

—GEORGE DOLAN in
Fort Worth Star-Telegram

While other people go to church every Sunday morning, Charles, a farmer, likes to sit in the village restaurant drinking wine.

One day the priest said to him, "Charles, I'm afraid we shall not see each other in heaven."

A worried Charles replied, "But, Father, what on earth have you done?"

—AIDA C. FUDOT

A preacher's new car broke down just after his Sunday service. Monday morning he managed to drive the vehicle to the town's one garage for repairs. "I hope you'll go easy on the cost," he told the mechanic. "After all, I'm just a poor preacher."

"I know," came the reply. "I heard you preach yesterday."

—*Lutheran Digest*

Unbeknown to most of the congregation, the new minister enjoyed an occasional bottle of wine. One church member, aware of this, presented the clergyman with a bottle of Bordeaux. But the gift had a string attached. The minister would have to say thank you from the pulpit.

At the conclusion of the next service, the minister made the announcements, then said, "And I want to thank my friend for giving the fine fruit, and for the spirit in which it was given."

—R. L. FINDLEY

A guru who claimed he survived on air started a cult. When some skeptics caught him munching a hamburger and french fries, the pseudo-psychic said, "You can't call this food."

—MARK PLUMMER in *The Indian Post*

You Should Die Laughing

Surprised to see an empty seat at the Super Bowl, a diehard fan remarked about it to a woman sitting nearby.

"It was my husband's," the woman explained, "but he died."

"I'm very sorry," said the man. "Yet I'm really surprised that another relative, or friend, didn't jump at the chance to take the seat reserved for him."

"Beats me," she said. "They all insisted on going to the funeral."

—*Coffee Break*

"Remember me? Bangor Maine. Moose season, 1971."

A young couple had a fatal car accident on the way to their wedding. When they met St. Peter at the Pearly Gates, they asked if it was possible for them to marry in heaven. He said he would make some inquiries and get back to them.

A year later, St. Peter found the couple and told them they could get married. "Could we get a divorce if it doesn't work out?" they wanted to know.

"Good grief!" St. Peter exclaimed. "It took me a whole year to find a preacher up here—and now you want me to find a lawyer."

—DEE MCDONALD

An attorney died and went to heaven. As he approached the Pearly Gates, he noticed an orchestra playing and thousands of angels cheering. St. Peter himself rushed over to shake the lawyer's hand. "This is quite a reception," marveled the new arrival.

"You're very special," St. Peter explained. "We've never had anyone live to be 130 before."

The attorney was puzzled. "But I'm only 65."

St. Peter thought for a moment. "Oh," he said, "we must have added up your billing hours."

—DAVID MICUS

When her late husband's will was read, a widow learned he had left the bulk of his fortune to another woman. Enraged, she rushed to change the inscription on her spouse's tombstone.

"Sorry, lady," said the stonecutter. "I inscribed 'Rest in Peace" on your orders. I can't change it now."

"Very well," she said grimly. "Just add 'Until We Meet Again.' "

—ROBERT E. CANTELL

Two ministers died and went to heaven. St. Peter greeted them and said, "Your condos aren't ready yet. Until they're finished, you can return to earth as anything you want."

"Fine," said the first minister. "I've always wanted to be an eagle soaring over the Grand Canyon."

"And I'd like to be a real cool stud," said the second.

Poof! Their wishes were granted.

When the condos were finished St. Peter asked an assistant to bring back the two ministers. "How will I find them?" the man said.

"One is soaring over the Grand Canyon," St. Peter replied. "The other may be tough to locate. He's somewhere in Detroit—on a snow tire."

—DONNA S. TIPTON

After a preacher died and went to heaven, he noticed that a New York cabdriver had been given a higher place than he had. "I don't understand," he complained to St. Peter. "I devoted my entire life to my congregation."

"Our policy is to reward results," explained St. Peter. "Now what happened, Reverend, whenever you gave a sermon?"

The minister admitted that some in the congregation fell asleep.

"Exactly," said St. Peter. "And when people rode in this man's taxi, they not only stayed awake, they *prayed*."

—Quoted by RAYMOND A. HEIT

Two guys, Jimmy and Johnny, were standing at heaven's gate, waiting to be interviewed by St. Peter.

Jimmy: "How did you get here?"

Johnny: "Hypothermia. You?"

Jimmy: "You won't believe it. I was sure my wife was cheating on me, so I came home early one day hoping to find the guy. I accused my wife of unfaithfulness and searched the whole house without any luck. Then I felt so bad about the whole thing I had a massive heart attack."

Johnny: "Oh, man, if you had checked the walk-in freezer, we'd both be alive."

—FAIZ RAHMAN

A man asked an acquaintance how his wife was; then, suddenly remembering that she had died, he blurted out, "Still in the same cemetery?"

—MAURO BORBA COLLETES ALVES

They say when you die you see bright light at the end of a tunnel," notes comedian Ed Marques. "I think my father will see the light, then flip it off to save electricity."

—*Comic Strip Live*, Fox TV

A gold miner died and went to heaven. At the gate, St. Peter asked, "What have you done in your life?"

When the man gave his occupation, St. Peter explained that there was already a surplus of miners in heaven. "May I stay if I get rid of the others?" the fellow inquired.

St. Peter agreed. Once in, the miner wandered around until he saw a couple of familiar faces. He whispered that there was a gold strike in hell. Soon, the place was empty of miners.

But a while later, the miner asked St. Peter for permission to leave. "Even if I did start the rumor," he said, "there just might be something to it!"

—Modern Gold Miner & Treasure Hunter

The day after Mrs. Zelkin's funeral, the rabbi dropped in to console the widower. To his astonishment he saw the bereaved on the sofa kissing a dazzling redhead.

"Zelkin!" roared the rabbi. "Your beloved wife is not even cold in her grave, and already you're—"

Mr. Zelkin cried, "In my grief, should I know what I'm doing?"

*—*LEO ROSTEN, *Hooray for Yiddish!*

Ninety-year-old Sam bought a hairpiece, had a face lift and worked out at the gym for six months. Then he found a widow half his age to take to dinner. As they got out of his sports car, Sam was struck by lightning and died. At the Gate of Heaven, he ran up to God and asked, "Why me?"

"Oh, Sam," replied God. "I didn't recognize you!"

*—*NANCY HARRISON

Overheard: "My greatest fear is that I will be standing behind Mother Teresa in the Final Judgment line and I'll hear God tell her, 'You know, you should have done more.'"

—The Jokesmith

"Sorry, bub. You're not in the database."

A Texas oilman died and went to heaven. After a few days, his bragging was getting on St. Peter's nerves. No matter what part of paradise he was shown, the oilman claimed it failed to measure up to Texas. Finally St. Peter took him to the edge of heaven so he could look straight into hell. "Have you got anything like that in Texas?" the saint demanded.

"No," the oilman replied. "But I know some ol' boys down in Houston who can put it out."

—DANA CONNER

St. Peter halted a man at the entrance to heaven. "You've told too many lies to be permitted in here," he said.

"Have a heart," replied the man. "Remember, you were once a fisherman yourself."

—HAROLD HELFER in *Catholic Digest*

An angel appears at a faculty meeting and tells the dean that in return for his unselfish and exemplary behavior, the Lord will reward him with his choice of infinite wealth, wisdom, or beauty. Without hesitating, the dean selects infinite wisdom.

"Done!" says the angel, and disappears in a cloud of smoke and a bolt of lightning. Now, all heads turn toward the dean, who sits surrounded by a faint halo of light. At length, one of his colleagues whispers, "Say something."

The dean sighs and says, "I should have taken the money."

—BETSY DEVINE and JOEL E. COHEN,
Absolute Zero Gravity

Three men died and went to heaven. Upon their arrival, St. Peter asked the first if he had been faithful to his wife. The man admitted to two affairs during his marriage. St. Peter told him that he could receive only a compact car to drive in heaven.

Then St. Peter asked the second man if he had been faithful to his wife, and the man admitted to one affair. St. Peter told him he would be given a midsize car to drive.

The third man was asked about his faithfulness, and he told St. Peter he had been true to his wife until the day he died. St. Peter praised him and gave him a luxury car.

A week later the three men were driving around, and they all stopped at a red light. The men in the compact and midsize cars turned to see the man in the luxury car crying. They asked him what could possibly be the matter—after all, he was driving a luxury car.

"I just passed my wife," he told them. "She was on a skateboard."

—BOBI GORIA

"That's it? 'Keep my head down'?"

Sports

Fast Pitches

The national pastime of Tahiti is making love," says Bob Hope. "But we, silly fools, picked baseball."

After the rookie pitcher walked a third straight batter, the manager strolled to the mound. "Son," he told the southpaw, "I think you've had enough."

"But look who's coming to bat," whined the rookie. "I struck this guy out the last time he was up."

"Yeah, I know," said the manager. "But this is still the same inning."

—*Sunshine* Magazine

During a baseball game, a woman kept shouting threats at the umpire. No matter what happened on the field, she continually yelled, "Kill the umpire!" This went on for an hour. "Lady," another fan called out, "the umpire hasn't done anything wrong."

"He's my husband," she replied. "Last night he came home with lipstick on his collar. Kill the umpire!"

—*Milton Berle's Private Joke File*

Robert Orben says: "My wife claims I'm a baseball fanatic. She says all I ever read about is baseball. All I ever talk about is baseball. All I ever think about is baseball. I told her she's way off base."

Pitchers say the split-finger fastball is like sex," writes George Will. "When it's good, it's terrific, and when it's bad, it's still pretty good."

—*Men at Work*

"My man called for a fastball and your man threw a slider."

A rookie pitcher was struggling at the mound, so the catcher walked up to have a talk with him. "I've figured out your problem," he told the young southpaw. "You always lose control at the same point in every game."

"When is that?"

"Right after the national anthem."

—JEFF MacNELLY, Tribune Media Services

I have to cut down on hot dogs and beer," one bleacher bum said to another.

"Why's that?"

"Can't you see? I'm starting to get a ballpark figure."

—*The American Legion Magazine*

The morning of a New York Mets game, a fan went to see if his tickets were still on the dashboard of his car. But he discovered that the windshield was smashed.

"Someone broke in and took our tickets?" asked his wife.

"Worse than that," the man replied. "Someone left four more."

—Quoted by JAMES DENT in the Charleston, W.Va., *Gazette*

Carl and Abe are two old baseball fanatics. They agree that whoever dies first will try to come back and tell the other one if there's baseball in heaven.

One evening Abe passes away in his sleep. A few nights later Carl hears what sounds like Abe's voice. "Abe, is that you?" he asks.

"Of course it's me," Abe replies.

"I can't believe it," Carl whispers. "So tell me, is there baseball in heaven?"

"Well, I have good news and bad news," Abe says. "The good news is, yes, there's baseball in heaven. The bad news is you're pitching tomorrow night."

—DAVID DANGLER

"I don't know, 'fore' hardly seems adequate."

Chasing the
Little White Ball

Jock and Angus, two craggy Scots, were sitting before the club-house fireplace after 18 holes on a raw, blustery day. The ice slowly melted from their beards and collected in puddles under their chairs. Outside, the wind howled off the North Sea and hail rattled against the windows.

The pair sat in silence over their whiskies. Finally Jock spoke: "Next Tuesday, same time?"

"Aye," Angus replied, "weather permittin'."

—MALCOLM MCNAIR in *Golf Illustrated*

"Are you my caddie?" asked the golfer.

"Yes, sir," replied the boy.

"And are you any good at finding lost balls?"

"Yes, sir."

"Right, then. Find one and let's start the game."

—STAN SAACKS

Three senior golfers were griping continually. "The fairways are too long," said one. "The hills are too high," said another. "The bunkers are too deep," complained the third.

Finally an 80-year-old put things into perspective. "At least," he noted, "we're on the right side of the grass."

—HAROLD L. WEAVER

When the legendary salesman was asked his secrets of success, he gave a humble shrug. "I'm sure you all know the cardinal rules: know your product; make lots of calls; never take no for an answer. But, honestly, I owe my success to consistently missing a three-foot putt by two inches."

—ASHTON APPLEWHITE, WILLIAM R. EVANS III, and ANDREW FROTHINGHAM, *And I Quote*

You can always spot an employee who's playing golf with his boss. He's the fellow who gets a hole in one and says, "Oops!"

—BOB MONKHOUSE, *Just Say a Few Words*

Did you hear about the politically correct country club? They no longer refer to their golfers as having handicaps. Instead they're "stroke challenged."

—*Comedy on Call*

Husband to wife: "You're always nagging me about my golf. It's driving me mad."

Wife: "It wouldn't be a drive—just a short putt."

—HARRY LEECH

A married couple, both avid golfers, were discussing the future one night. "Honey," the wife said, "if I were to die and you were to remarry, would you two live in this house?"

"I suppose so—it's paid for."

"How about our car?" continued the woman. "Would the two of you keep that?"

"I suppose so—it's paid for."

"What about my golf clubs? Would you let her use them too?"

"Heck, no," the husband blurted out. "She's left-handed."

—DON CRIQUI on Imus in the Morning, WFAN, New York

A man played golf every Saturday and always got home around 2:00 in the afternoon. One Saturday, however, he rushed in at 7:30 PM and blurted to his wife, "I left the course at the normal time, but on the way home I stopped to change a flat tire for a young woman. She offered to buy me a drink, one thing led to another, and we spent the entire afternoon in a motel. I'm so sorry. I'll never do it again."

"Don't hand me that malarkey," the angry wife shouted. "You played 36 holes, didn't you?"

—GEORGE W. EDWARDS

Did you hear about Fred trying to drown himself in the water hazard on the tenth hole?" a weekend golfer asked his partner.

"No kidding!" said the other duffer. "What happened?"

"Nothing, really. He couldn't keep his head down there either."

—Quoted by ED BAER on The Ed Baer Affair,
WHUD, Peekskill, N.Y.

Two male golfers were held up by two women players ahead, so one went forward to ask if they could play through.

He returned, looking embarrassed, and explained, "I couldn't speak to them—one is my wife, and the other is my mistress."

His partner then went forward, only to return muttering, "What an extraordinary coincidence!"

—L. D. TURNER

Marooned on a South Seas island, a man with a beard down to his knees is walking on the beach. Suddenly a beautiful woman emerges from the surf.

"Been here long?" she asks.

"Since 1981," he replies.

"How long has it been since you've had a cigarette?"

"Eleven years."

She unzips a pocket in the sleeve of her wet suit, pulls out a pack of Camels, lights one, and hands it to him. He inhales greedily. "How long since you've had a drink of whiskey?"

"Eleven years."

She unzips the other sleeve and offers him a flask. He takes a long pull and looks at her adoringly.

"How long," she asks coyly, "since you played around?"

"Eleven years," he says wistfully.

She starts to unzip the front of her wet suit. "Gosh," he says, "you got a set of golf clubs in there?"

—NED PARKER, quoted by ALEX THIEN
in the Milwaukee *Sentinel*

What's your handicap these days?" one golfer asked another.

"I'm a scratch golfer. . . . I write down all my good scores and scratch out all my bad ones."

—CHARLES SCHULZ, United Features Syndicate

"I told you this was rough hole!"

Mack the Slice, a notorious duffer, unwound on the first tee and sent a high drive far to the right. The ball sailed through an open window. Figuring that was the end of it, Mack played on.

On the eighth hole, a police officer walked up to Mack and asked, "Did you hit a ball through that window?"

"Yes, I did."

"Well, it knocked a lamp over, scaring the dog, which raced out of the house onto the highway. A driver rammed into a brick wall to avoid the dog, sending three people to the hospital. And all because you sliced the ball."

"I'm so sorry," moaned Mack. "Is there anything I can do?"

"Well," the cop replied, "try keeping your head down and close up your stance a bit."

—BILL MAJESKI in *Catholic Digest*

Golfer: "What's your handicap?"
Second golfer: "Honesty."

—*Executive Speechwriter Newsletter*

The minister was on the golf course when he heard a duffer, deep in a sand trap, let loose a stream of profanity. "I have often noticed," chided the minister, "that the best golfers are not addicted to the use of foul language."

"Of course not," screamed the man. "What do they have to swear about?"

—*Contact*

She: "How'd your doctor appointment go?"
He: "Well, there's good news and bad news. My blood pressure's high and I'm overweight. But, at the doctor's suggestion, I'm going to take up golf!"
She: "And the good news?"

—GREG EVANS, North American Syndicate

First golfer: "I have the greatest golf ball in the world. You can't lose it."

Second golfer: "How so?"

First golfer: "If you hit it into the sand, it beeps. You hit it into the water, it floats. If you want to play golf at night, it glows."

Second golfer: "Hey, sounds good. Where did you get it?"

First golfer: "Found it in the woods."

—BYRON SMIALEK in the
Washington, Pa., *Observer-Reporter*

Honey, I have a confession to make," a guy told his bride. "I'm a golf nut. You'll never see me on weekends during golf season."

"Well, dear," she murmured. "I have a confession to make too. I'm a hooker."

"No big deal," replied the groom. "Just keep your head down and your left arm straight."

—JAY TRACHMAN in *One to One*

Fish Tales and Hunting Licenses

Question: What's the difference between a hunter and a fisherman?

Answer: A hunter lies in wait while a fisherman waits and lies.

—*One to One*

A fisherman accidentally left his day's catch under the seat of a bus. The next evening's newspaper carried an ad: "If the person who left a bucket of fish on the No. 47 bus would care to come to the garage, he can have the bus."

—Sri Lanka *Sunday Island*

*"Your father, may he rest in peace, was
considered quite a catch."*

Simon was an inveterate fisherman, well known for exaggerating the size of "the one that got away." But there came a day when he actually caught two enormous flounders. He immediately invited a few friends over to dine, then tried to figure out how best to serve the fish. "If I use both," he told his wife, "it will seem ostentatious."

"Why not serve a piece of each?" she suggested.

"No, if I cut them up, nobody will believe I caught two giant flounders." Simon racked his brain. Then he had an idea.

The guests were seated at the table when their host strode in with a platter, holding the biggest flounder they'd ever seen. Suddenly Simon stumbled and fell. Everyone cried out in dismay as the fish crashed to the floor, but Simon quickly brushed himself off.

"Dear," he called out to his wife, "bring in the other flounder!"

—HENRY D. SPALDING, *Jewish Laffs*

An optimist who went hunting with a pessimist wanted to show off his new dog. After the first shot, he sent his dog to fetch a duck. The dog ran across the top of the water and brought back the game. The pessimist said nothing. The dog retrieved the second and third ducks the same way—over the water. Still the pessimist did not react. Finally, the optimist could stand it no longer. "Don't you see anything unusual about my new dog?" he asked his companion.

"Yes—he can't swim."

—BOB PHILLIPS quoted by MARTHA BOLTON,
"If Mr. Clean Calls, Tell Him I'm Not In!"

Two would-be fishermen rented a boat, and one caught a large fish. "We should mark the spot," he said. The other man drew a large X in the bottom of the boat with a black marker.

"That's no good," said the first man. "Next time out we may not get the same boat."

—FLORENCE KILLAM

A hunting party was hopelessly lost. "I thought you said you were the best guide in Maine!" one of the hunters angrily said to their confused leader.

"I am," replied the guide. "But I think we're in Canada now."

—*Reminisce*

A New South Wales fisherman lost his dentures over the side of the boat in rough weather, so his prankster friend removed his own false teeth, tied them on his line and pretended he had caught the missing gnashers.

Unhooking the teeth, his grateful mate tried to put them into his mouth, then hurled them into the sea with the disgusted remark: "They're not mine—they don't fit!"

—"Column 8,"
The Sydney Morning Herald

Two Texans went up to Minnesota to go ice fishing. After setting up their tent, they started to cut a hole in the ice. As they pulled the cord on their chain saw, they heard a voice from above: "There are no fish under the ice."

When they pulled the cord again, the same voice intoned: "There are no fish under the ice."

"Is that you, God?" they asked in awe.

"No," came the reply. "I own this ice rink—and I can tell you that there are no fish under the ice."

—N. E. Dunnuck

While hunting, Larry and Elmer got lost in the woods. Trying to reassure his friend, Larry said, "Don't worry. All we have to do is shoot into the air three times, stay where we are, and someone will find us."

They shot in the air three times, but no one came. After a while, they tried it again. Still no response. When they decided to try once more, Elmer said, "It better work this time. We're down to our last three arrows."

—Elizabeth Clark

The tale is told of Boudreaux, out on the bayou, fishing by dropping sticks of dynamite over the side, waiting for the "boom" and scooping the fish out with a net. After he'd done this four or five times, the game warden came out and said, "Boudreaux, you know you ain't s'posed to be fishin' that way."

Boudreaux paid him no mind. Lighting up another stick of dynamite, he handed it to the game warden and said, "You gonna talk or you gonna fish?"

—Dennis R. Edwards

"I think he's had it as a bird dog."

A group of friends who went deer hunting separated into pairs for the day. That night, one hunter returned alone, staggering under an eight-point buck. "Where's Harry?" asked another hunter.

"He fainted a couple miles up the trail," Harry's partner answered.

"You left him lying there alone and carried the deer back?"

"A tough call," said the hunter. "But I figured no one is going to steal Harry."

—*The Jokesmith*

An American had been fishing for two weeks in Ireland without getting a bite. On the last day of his vacation, he caught a small salmon.

"Turlough," he said to his guide later, "that salmon cost me more than five hundred dollars."

"Well now, sir," Turlough comforted him, "aren't you lucky you didn't catch two!"

—IAN AITKEN

After a long day of fishing without even a nibble, a man said disgustedly to his companion, "You know the saying, 'Give a man a fish, and he'll eat for a day; teach a man to fish, and he'll eat for a lifetime'?"

"Yes?"

"Well, whoever said it wasn't a fisherman."

—DAVID SAHLIN

Irving was boasting to a fellow fisherman about a 20-pound salmon he had caught. "Twenty pounds, huh?" remarked the other guy, with skepticism. "Were there any witnesses?"

"Of course," said Irving. "Otherwise it would have weighed 30 pounds."

—JOEY ADAMS

The young boy protested vigorously when his mother asked him to take his little sister along fishing. "The last time she came," he objected, "I didn't catch a single fish."

"I'll talk to her," his mother said, "and I promise this time she won't make any noise."

"It wasn't the noise, Mom," the boy replied. "She ate all my bait."

—*The Rotarian*

Three men were sitting on a park bench. The one in the middle was reading a newspaper; the others were pretending to fish. They baited imaginary hooks, cast lines, and reeled in their catch.

A passing policeman stopped to watch the spectacle and asked the man in the middle if he knew the other two.

"Oh yes," he said. "They're my friends."

"In that case," warned the officer, "you'd better get them out of here!"

"Yes, sir," the man replied, and he began rowing furiously.

—ADAM T. RATTRAY

Said a fisherman after removing a tiny fish from his hook and throwing it back into the water: "Don't show up around here anymore without your parents!"

—*Der Stern*

The novice ice fisherman wasn't having any luck, but another man nearby was pulling up fish after fish through the ice. "What's your secret?" the newcomer asked.

"Mmnpximdafgltmm," mumbled the man.

"I'm sorry, I couldn't understand you," said the novice.

"Mmnpximdafgltmm!" the fisherman mumbled again.

The neophyte shook his head and began to turn away, when the other man held up his hand. Spitting twice into his coffee cup, he said, "You've got to keep the worms warm!"

—BRIAN D. HOXIE

Sitting in a rowboat, the novice fisherman asked his companion, "Got any more of those little plastic floats?"

"Why?"

"This one keeps sinking."

—ART SANSOM, Newspaper Enterprise Assn.

Three statisticians go deer hunting with bows and arrows. They spot a big buck and take aim. One shoots, and his arrow flies off 10 feet to the left. The second shoots, and his arrow goes 10 feet to the right. The third statistician jumps up and down yelling, "We got him! We got him!"

—BILL BUTZ, quoted by DIANA MCLELLAN in
Washingtonian

You Must Be Jock-ing!

Before a major college basketball game between two top-20 teams, one student nudged another and said, "Look at that player. I wonder what's the matter with him. He looks so depressed."

"You haven't heard?" asked the other. "It's because his father's always writing him for money!"

—*Ideas for Better Living*

Basketball sure is an amazing game," said one fan to another. "They pay a guy $500,000 a year to shoot the ball, and then they call it a free throw."

—JAY TRACHMAN in *One to One*

He's great on the court," a sportswriter said of a college basketball player in an interview with his coach. "But how's his scholastic work?"

"Why, he makes straight A's," replied the coach.

"Wonderful!" said the sportswriter.

"Yes," agreed the coach, "but his B's are a little crooked."

—CLARENCE PETERSEN in the
Jacksonville, Fla., *Times-Union*

"He's what I call a natural."

An avid Dallas Cowboys fan took his dog to a sports bar one Sunday afternoon to watch the game. The bartender reluctantly let the dog in, and the pooch sat quietly as the game progressed. When the Cowboys got a field goal, the dog went crazy—barking, running in circles and doing back flips. "What does he do when they score a touchdown?" the amazed bartender asked.

"I don't know," replied the owner. "I've only had him two years."
—Contributed by HOWARD R. SCHROEDER

After spending all day watching football, Harry fell asleep in front of the TV and spent the night in the chair. In the morning, his wife woke him up. "Get up, dear," she said. "It's 20 to seven."

He awoke with a start. "In whose favor?"

—Funny, Funny World

A college football coach had recruited a top talent, but the player couldn't pass the school's entrance exam. Needing the recruit badly, the coach went to the dean and asked if the recruit could take the test orally. The dean agreed, and the following day the recruit and the coach were seated in his office. "Okay," the dean said. "What is seven times seven?"

The recruit mulled it over for a moment, then said, "I think it's 49."

Suddenly the coach leapt to his feet. "Please, Dean," he begged, "give him another chance!"

—Oscar Zimmerman

Mort Sahl sympathized with football widows. When one woman asked him how she could get her husband's attention away from the TV set, he said, "Wear something sheer."

"What if that doesn't work?" she asked.

"Then put a number on your back," Sahl replied.

—Joey Adams

What position does your brother play on the football team?" Tom was asked.

"I'm not real sure," the boy replied, "but I think he's one of the drawbacks."

—Quoted in the
Milwaukee *Journal*

P.C. VEY

Anthropologists have discovered a 50-million-year-old human skull with three perfectly preserved teeth intact. They're not sure, but they think it may be the remains of the very first hockey player.

—JAY LENO

The 85-year-old woman decided to take up skydiving. After she attended instruction classes, the day came for her first jump. Strapping on a parachute, she stood awaiting her turn to leap out of the plane. But when she looked at the ground below, she lost her nerve.

Finally, she reached into her pocket, pulled out a small transmitter and radioed her instructor on the ground: "Help! I've gotten up, and I can't fall down!"

—KEN BEHRENS,
WJBC, Bloomington, Ill.

Young woman to boyfriend:

"Otto, you'd really rather watch soccer than me?"

"Yes," he says apologetically. "But I'd take you any day over the long jump, swimming, and the equestrian contest."

—ANDREA RATONYI

Bill and George were always competing against each other. After one argument over who was better at folding and packing parachutes, they went skydiving to settle the dispute. Bill jumped first, pulled the cord and began to float gently to earth. Then George jumped and pulled his cord, but nothing happened. Next he yanked on the safety cord, but that didn't work either. In a matter of seconds George, falling like a rock, flew past Bill. "So," Bill shouted, ripping off his harness, "you want to race!"

—MARIE THRUSH

A sky diver and his instructor peered down at the field 3,000 feet below. "There's nothing to worry about," the instructor said. "You jump, count to three and pull your rip cord. If that doesn't work, pull your reserve cord. There'll be a truck down there to pick you up."

The sky diver took a deep breath and plunged into the open air. After free-falling, he counted to three, then pulled his rip cord. Nothing happened. So he pulled his reserve. A few cobwebs drifted out.

"Darn," he said. "I'll bet that truck's not down there either."

—*Playboy*

Horsefeathers

The cavalryman was galloping down the road, rushing to catch up with his regiment. Suddenly his horse stumbled and pitched him to the ground. In the dirt with a broken leg, terrified of the approaching enemy, the soldier called out: "All you saints in heaven, help me get up on my horse!"

Then, with superhuman effort, he leaped onto the horse's back and fell off the other side. Once again on the ground, he called to the heavens: "All right, just half of you this time!"

—MRS. JAMES LARKIN

My wife means to lose weight. That's why she rides horseback all the time."

"And what's the result?"

"The horse lost 10 kilos last week."

—M. SPIRKOV

Overheard at the track: "Horse racing is very romantic. The horse hugs the rail, the jockey puts his arms around the horse, and you kiss your money good-bye."

—SACHIN MATADE

About to take his first horseback ride, the greenhorn was checking out the horses in the stable. The old wrangler asked whether he wanted an English saddle or a Western saddle.

"What's the difference?" asked the tenderfoot.

"The English saddle is flat, while the Western has a horn in the front."

"Better give me the English saddle," the fellow replied. "I don't expect to be riding in traffic."

—R. J. LANDSEADEL JR. in *The Rotarian*

Gasping for breath and covered with sweat, a man came into a racetrack snack bar and ordered a soft drink. "What happened to you?" the waitress asked.

"I was in the paddock area," the man panted, "when I saw a $100 bill on the ground. I bent down to pick it up. While I was bent over, somebody threw a saddle on me, and a jockey jumped into the saddle. The next thing I knew, I was on the track and the jockey was whipping my flanks."

"No kidding?" said the surprised woman. "What did you do?"

"I finished third."

—JERRY H. SIMPSON JR.

An elderly gentleman went to a dude ranch and asked for the rates. "Well," began the ranch director, "for people your age who can't handle horses very well, we have to charge an extra 50 dollars a day."

"Fifty dollars a day!" yelped the old-timer. "You must be putting me on!"

"No," explained the director. "That would be an additional 20 dollars."

—ASHLEY COOPER in Charleston, S.C., *News and Courier*

A man was walking down a country road when he heard a voice coming from behind a tree, but all he could see was a horse.

"Hello, remember me?" the voice said. "I won the Kentucky Derby two years ago."

"A talking horse!" the man exclaimed, so he rushed to a nearby field where the farmer was working and asked, "What would you take for the horse?"

"That darned horse is no good, you can have him for 20 dollars."

"Twenty dollars! I'll give you 2,000."

"Has that old haybag been giving you that baloney about winning the Kentucky Derby? Listen, I happen to know he came in last."

—*The Carpenter*

"Mom? Dad? Who are these people?."

Entertainment

**ROAR OF THE GREASEPAINT,
SMELL OF THE CROWD! 108**

WAITER! WAITER! 114

HAPPY HOUR 119

YOU BETCHA' 123

WITH A RUB OF THE LAMP 126

Roar of the Greasepaint, Smell of the Crowd

If he starts to cry, you'll have to leave the theater," a movie-theater usher warned a young couple with an infant, "but you can ask for your money back."

Thirty minutes into the film, the husband whispered to his wife, "What do you think?"

"This film is a waste of time."

"I agree. Why not wake the baby up?"

—CARINE SCHENKEL

Sam: "I used to be a stand-up comedian before I worked here."
Joe: "I never would have guessed that."
Sam: "Ask me why I quit."
Joe: "Why did you ..."
Sam: "Timing!"
Joe: "...quit?"

—MIKE SMITH

As the man and wife returned to their seats in the dark auditorium, the husband asked a fellow seated on the aisle, "Did someone step on your feet while going out at intermission?"

"Yes, *you* did," he replied, expecting an apology.

"Okay, honey," the man said to his wife, "this is our row."

—DUKE LARSON, quoted by Alex Thien
in the Milwaukee *Sentinel*

In Chicago there's a new Al Capone theme park. The commercial says, "Come to the park, pay your money, and nobody gets hurt."

—JOE HOBBY

When Disneyland celebrated its 40th anniversary, Disney officials buried a time capsule," reports Jay Leno. "They say it will be dug up in 50 years—or when the last person in line at Space Mountain gets to the front, whichever comes first."

A movie producer was telling his pal about giving his fiancée a string of pearls for her birthday. "Why," asked his friend, "don't you give her something practical—like a car?"

The producer answered, "Did you ever hear of a phony automobile?"

—*Another Treasury of Clean Jokes*, edited by TAL D. BONHAM

You're blocking the way, sir," said the usher to a man sprawled in the aisle of a movie theater. "Please get up."

The man didn't move or reply. The usher called the manager over, who said, "I must ask you to move."

Still the prone man didn't reply. So the manager called the police. "Get up or I'll have to take you in," the officer said. "Where did you come from anyway?"

The man stirred finally and said, "The balcony."

—*Capper's*

Browsing at a video shop, a guy and a gal spot the last tape of a recent hit movie. He grabs it first. "Your VCR or mine?" he asks.

—BILL COPELAND in the Sarasota, Fla., *Herald-Tribune*

Hollywood is the land of make-believe. Actors pretend they're someone else, and when the movie's finished, the producers make believe it's good.

—*Current Comedy*

"It's perfectly normal for your last film to flash before your eyes on Oscar night."

A Hollywood screenwriter coming home from work spotted a police line at the end of his street. He quickly discovered the reason: His house had burned to the ground. "What happened?" he asked a cop who was posted there.

"I'm sorry," the police officer said, "but your agent came over this afternoon and kidnapped your wife and children and then torched your house."

The screenwriter looked stunned. "My agent came to my *house*?"

—Esquire

Two Hollywood execs were overheard at a power breakfast. "You're *lying* to me!" shouted one, pounding the table.

"I know. You're right," said the other. "But hear me out."

—Quoted by JEFF GILES in *Newsweek*

In a darkened theater where a suspenseful mystery story was being staged, a member of the audience suddenly stood up and cried, "Where is the murderer?"

A threatening voice behind her replied, "Right in back of you, if you don't sit down!"

—PIERRE LÉAUTÉ

Movie cowboys mystify me," says Bob Hope. "How can they jump off a porch roof and onto a horse, and still sing in a normal voice?"

When I came to this country," writes comedian Yakov Smirnoff, "one of the toughest things to get used to was all the different names of rock bands like Ratt, the Grateful Dead, or Twisted Sister. Then I *saw* the people in these groups, and it began to make sense."

—America on Six Rubles a Day

They were watching a TV soap opera, and he became irritated by the way his wife was taking it to heart. "How can you sit there and cry about the made-up troubles of people you've never even met?" he demanded.

"The same way you can jump up and scream when some guy you've never met scores a touchdown," she replied.

—KRIS LEE in *Woman's World*

You know you're getting old when you walk into a record store and everything you like has been marked down to $1.99.

—JACK SIMMONS, *Showtime Comedy Cable*

A quiz program contestant had to identify famous slogans. After several correct responses, he was asked, "Which company originated the phrase 'Good to the last drop'?"

He thought for a moment. "Otis Elevator?"

—JACK TRACY

Mel's son rushed in the door. "Dad! Dad!" he announced. "I got a part in the school play!"

"That's terrific," Mel said proudly. "What part is it?"

"I play the part of the dad."

Mel thought this over. "Go back tomorrow," he instructed, "and tell them you want a speaking role."

—DARLEEN GIANNINI

When a plague of flying ants caused the performance at a variety theater in the Australian outback to end prematurely, the manager cabled a message to his agent: "Show stopped by flying ants!"

"Book 'em for another week," replied the agent.

—BOB BROADFIELD

• •

A stage mother cornered the concert violinist in his dressing room and insisted he listen to a tape of her talented son playing the violin. The man agreed to listen, and the woman switched on the tape player.

What music, the violinist thought. A difficult piece, but played with such genius that it brought tears to his eyes. He listened spellbound to the entire recording.

"Madam," he whispered, "is that your son?"

"No," she replied. "That's Jascha Heifetz. But my son sounds just like him."

—*The Jokesmith*

Overheard: "I had a disturbing discussion with my wife this morning. I said that men like Sylvester Stallone and Arnold Schwarzenegger are a dime a dozen. She said, 'Here's a nickel. Get me six!' "

—*Current Comedy*

A couple of extras in the play were talking backstage at the end of the performance. "What's the matter with our leading lady?" one actress asked. "She seems really mad about something."

"Oh, she's upset because she only received nine bouquets of flowers over the footlights," the other woman answered.

"Nine!" exclaimed the first actress. "That's pretty good, isn't it?"

"Yes," her friend replied, "but she paid for 10."

—*The Safe Way*

Did you hear about the $2.7-billion write-off Sony took on its Hollywood studio? "That was quick!" says comedy writer Michael Connor. "It took the Japanese only a couple of years to master Hollywood-style bookkeeping."

—*The Los Angeles Times*

Waiter! Waiter!

Waiter," Billy roars in the restaurant. "I want a steak, but it must taste just like veal. In the soup there must be no more and no less than 16 droplets of fat, and the wine must be served at exactly 50 degrees. The crystal wineglass must sound in A-flat when I tap it."

The waiter remains stoically calm, notes down every request, and then asks: "And the toothpicks, sir? Would you like them to be Rococo, Biedermier, Jugendstil, or would you prefer something in a slightly more modern line?"

—URBAIN KOOPMANS

When the waitress in a New York City restaurant brought him the soup du jour, the Englishman was a bit dismayed. "Good heavens," he said, "what is this?"

"Why, it's bean soup," she replied.

"I don't care what it has been," he sputtered. "What is it now?"

—MARGARET OLDEROG

The diner was furious when his steak arrived too rare. "Waiter," he barked, "didn't you hear me say 'well done'?"

"I can't thank you enough, sir," replied the waiter. "I hardly ever get a compliment."

—A. H. BERZEN

A diner called the waiter over and asked, "What's this at the bottom of my plate?"

"It's the design," replied the waiter.

"In that case," said the diner, "it's an animated drawing—it's moving!"

—*Humor Piadas e Anedotas*

"I realize we all look alike, sir, but I am Walter, a married man with two grown children, and an abiding interest in the theater, coin collecting, and small songbirds. Your waiter is Eddie. I'll send him over."

In a restaurant where the service was particularly slow, a customer was fretting because the waiter had not taken his order, although he had been waiting for a quarter of an hour. When the waiter finally appeared at his table, bearing a small dish of peanuts, he found the place empty, except for a small note from the disappointed diner: "Gone out to lunch!"

—MINA and ANDRÉ GUILLOIS

The truck driver looked askance at the soup he had just been served in a backwoods eatery. It contained dark flecks of seasoning, but two of the spots were suspicious.

"Hey," he called out to the waitress, "these particles in my soup—aren't they foreign objects?"

She scrutinized his bowl. "No, sir!" she reassured him. "Those things live around here."

—DEAN MORGAN

A patron in a Montreal café turned on a tap in the washroom and got scalded. "This is an outrage," he complained. "The faucet marked C gave me boiling water."

"But, Monsieur, C stands for *chaude*—French for hot. You should know that if you live in Montreal."

"Wait a minute," roared the patron. "The other tap is also marked C."

"Of course," said the manager. "It stands for cold. After all, Montreal is a bilingual city."

—*Catholic Digest*

My family and I were eating in an expensive restaurant, when I overheard the gentleman at the next table ask the waitress to pack the leftovers for their dog. It was then that his young son exclaimed loudly, "Whoopee! We're going to get a dog."

—B. S. PRABHAKAR

How many cups of coffee will this hold?" the man asked as he placed a large thermos on the lunch-room counter.

"Six cups," advised the waitress.

"Fine," replied the man. "Give me two cups regular, two cups black, and two with extra cream."

—GEORGE E. BERGMAN

● ●

The disgruntled diner summoned his waiter to the table, complaining, "My oyster stew doesn't have any oysters in it."

"Well, if that bothers you, then you better skip dessert," replied the waiter. "It's angel food cake."

—ROBERT L. RODGERS

Ours is a good restaurant," said the manager. "If you order an egg, you get the freshest egg in the world. If you order hot coffee, you get the hottest coffee in the world, and—"

"I believe you," said the customer. "I ordered a small steak."

—JIM REED, *Treasury of Ozark Country Humor*

A man walked into a crowded New York City restaurant and caught the eye of a harried waiter. "You know," he said, "it's been 10 years since I came in here."

"Don't blame me," the waiter snapped. "I'm working as fast as I can."

—NORTON MOCKRIDGE, United Features Syndicate

Inflation is creeping up," a young man said to his friend. "Yesterday I ordered a $25 steak in a restaurant and told them to put it on my American Express card—and it fit."

—DON REBER in the Reading, Pa., *Times*

Two eggs were in a pot, being boiled. One said to the other, "It's so hot in here I don't think I can stand it much longer."

The other replied, "Don't grumble. As soon as they get you out of here, they bash your head in with a spoon."

—J. JONES

"My, oh, my! What a fascinating guy you are, Vincent! But now, if it's not too much trouble, I'd like you to take my order."

The big Texan, visiting New York for the first time, entered a fancy restaurant and ordered a steak. The waiter served it very rare. The Texan took one look at it and demanded that it be returned to the kitchen and cooked.

"It is cooked," snapped the waiter.

"Cooked—nothing!" shouted the Texan. "I've seen cows hurt worse than that get well."

—H. B. McClung

In a greasy spoon, a downhearted diner asked the waitress for meatloaf and some kind words. She brought the meatloaf but didn't say a thing. "Hey," he said, "what about my kind words?"

She replied, "Don't eat the meatloaf."

—*The Los Angeles Times*

Happy Hour

While at the pub, an Englishman, an Irishman, and a Scot each found a fly swimming around in his beer. The Englishman asked the bartender for a napkin and a teaspoon. Elegantly scooping the fly out, he placed it in the napkin and delicately folded it.

The Irishman pushed his sleeve up, immersed his hand in the beer, caught the fly, threw it on the floor, and stepped on it.

The Scot silently took his jacket off, draped it neatly over the chair, folded his shirtsleeves up, and bent over his pint. Carefully he fished the fly out by picking it up by its wings. He lifted it just above the mug, shook the fly, and in a threatening voice bellowed, "Now spit it out!"

—HANS J. GERHARDT

A college professor walked into a bar and said, "Bring me a martinus." The bartender smiled and said, "You mean martini?"

"If I want more than one," snapped the professor, "I'll order them."

—EARL WILSON

A grasshopper walks into a bar. The bartender looks at him and says, "Hey, they named a drink after you!"

"Really?" replies the grasshopper. "There's a drink named Stan?"

—FAYE SKULBERSTAD

At a party the hostess served a guest a cup of punch and told him it was spiked. Next, she served some to a minister. "I would rather commit adultery than allow liquor to pass my lips!" he shouted.

Hearing this, the first man poured his punch back and said, "I didn't know we had a choice!"

—DARRELL B. THOMPSON

Mike had stopped off at a small-town tavern and made his way to the bar when there was a commotion outside. A man at the door shouted, "Run for your lives! Big Jake's comin'!" As everyone scattered, an enormous man burst through the door, threw tables and chairs aside and strode up to the bar. "Gimme a drink!" he ordered.

Left alone at the bar, Mike quickly handed over a bottle of whiskey. The huge man downed it in one gulp, then ate the bottle. Paralyzed with fear, Mike stammered, "Can I g-get you another?"

"Nope, I gotta go," grunted the giant. "Didn't you hear? Big Jake's comin'!"

—HOWARD CHAVEZ

A fellow went to a bar and ordered a drink. He gulped it down and, to the amazement of the bartender, also ate the goblet, except for the stem. He ordered another, swallowed the drink, and again ate the goblet, leaving the stem. The bartender then called in a psychiatrist, explained the man's strange behavior, and asked whether he thought the man was eccentric. "He must be," the shrink replied. "The stem's the best part."

—P. R. ENGELE

A man walked into a second-story bar and ordered a drink. The man next to him began a conversation about wind currents in the area. The first man said he didn't understand what was so special about the wind, so the second man said, "Let me demonstrate."

With that, he went to the window, jumped out, did a little spin in midair and came back in. "See how great the currents are? You can do the same thing."

After a few more drinks and much prodding, the first man decided to test the wind currents. He went to the window, jumped out, and fell to the ground.

The bartender looked at the other man and said, "Superman, you're really mean when you're drunk."

—DARLEEN GIANNINI

Pat Muldoon, proprietor of an Irish pub, was busy pouring for his noontime trade, while trying to keep a swarm of flies away from the buffet table. When Mike Callahan, the town drunk and biggest mooch, wandered in, Pat turned a deaf ear to his plea for a nip or two on the cuff.

But when Mike offered to kill every one of the flies circling the buffet in exchange for a short one, Pat slid a shot of whiskey across the bar. As soon as he downed it, Mike rolled up his sleeves and headed for the door. "All right, Muldoon," he said. "Send 'em out one at a time."

—GORDON H. KRUEGER

A businesswoman is sitting at a bar. A man approaches her.
"Hi, honey," he says. "Want a little company?"
"Why?" asks the woman. "Do you have one to sell?"

—Quoted by CAROLYN A. STRADLEY

Late one night, after an evening of drinking, Smitty took a shortcut through the graveyard and stumbled into a newly dug grave. He could not get out, so he lay at the bottom and fell asleep. Early next morning the old caretaker heard moans and groans coming from deep in the earth. He went over to investigate, saw the shivering figure at the bottom and demanded, "What's wrong with ya, that you're makin' all that noise?"

"Oh, I'm awful cold!" came the response.

"Well, it's no wonder," said the caretaker. "You've gone and kicked all the dirt off ya!"

—DEBBIE P. WRIGHT

Overheard: "The police in this town have a very tough sobriety test. Not only do they make you blow up a balloon, but then you have to twist it into a giraffe."

—*Current Comedy*

"You guys know the rules! No discussing politics during happy hour."

A bar owner locked up his place at 2 AM and went home to sleep. He had been in bed only a few minutes when the phone rang. "What time do you open up in the morning?" he heard an obviously inebriated man inquire.

The owner was so furious, he slammed down the receiver and went back to bed. A few minutes later there was another call and he heard the same voice ask the same question. "Listen," the owner shouted, "there's no sense in asking me what time I open because I wouldn't let a person in your condition in—"

"I don't want to get in," the caller interjected. "I want to get *out*."

—*The Carpenter*

You Betcha'

Las Vegas is loaded with all kinds of gambling devices," says Joey Adams. "Dice tables, slot machines, and wedding chapels."

A woman in Atlantic City was losing at the roulette wheel. When she was down to her last 10 dollars, she asked the fellow next to her for a good number. "Why don't you play your age?" he suggested.

The woman agreed, and then put her money on the table. The next thing the fellow with the advice knew, the woman had fainted and fallen to the floor. He rushed right over. "Did she win?" he asked.

"No," replied the attendant. "She put 10 dollars on 29 and 41 came in."

—Christine L. Castner

In Las Vegas a big-time gambler dies and a friend delivers the eulogy. "Tony isn't dead," the friend says. "He only sleeps."

A mourner in the back of the room jumps up. "I got a hundred bucks says he's dead!"

—*Solutions for Seniors*

When Salley O'Malley of County Clare won the Irish Sweepstakes, she decided to treat herself to some of the finer things in life. "I've nivver had a milk bath," she told her milkman one morning. "Wouldja be bringin' me 96 quarts o' milk tomorro'?"

"Whativver ye want, mum," answered the milkman. "Will that be pasteurized?"

"No," said she. "Up to me chest will do."

—Quoted by T. D.

Sitting by the window in her convent, Sister Eulalia opened a letter from home, and found a $10 bill inside. As she read the letter, she caught sight of a shabbily dressed stranger leaning against a lamppost below. Quickly she wrote "Don't despair, Sister Eulalia" on a piece of paper, wrapped the $10 in it and dropped it out the window.

The stranger picked it up and, with a puzzled expression and a tip of his hat, went off down the street.

The next day Sister Eulalia was told that a man was at the door, insisting on seeing her. She went down and found the stranger waiting. Without a word he handed her a roll of bills. "What's this?" she asked.

"That's the 60 bucks you have coming. Don't Despair paid five to one."

—*The Joy of Words*

Bill sat at the local bar, bragging about his athletic prowess. None of the regulars challenged him, but a visitor piped up, "I'll bet you 50 bucks that I can push something in a wheelbarrow for one block and you can't wheel it back."

Bill looked over at the skinny stranger and decided it wasn't much of a challenge. "I'll take you on," he said.

The two men and a number of regulars borrowed a wheelbarrow and took it to the corner. "Now, let's see what you're made of," taunted Bill.

"Okay," said the challenger. "Get in."

—ANNE VICTORIA BAYNAS, quoted in
Old Farmer's Almanac

I'm beginning to understand exactly how the state lottery helps education," a guy told his neighbor. "Every time I buy a losing ticket, I get a little smarter."

—*One to One*

"I understand there are no slot machines in the original."

What are you so happy about?" a woman asked the 98-year-old man.

"I broke a mirror," he replied.

"But that means seven years of bad luck."

"I know," he said, beaming. "Isn't it wonderful?"

—BOB MONKHOUSE, *Just Say a Few Words*

Did you hear about the race horse that was so late coming in, they had to pay the jockey time and a half?
                    —TOM FITZGERALD in the San Francisco *Chronicle*

A confirmed horse player hadn't been to church in years even though his wife attended every week. One Sunday, however, he finally went with her.

"That wasn't so bad," he said on the way home. "The church was air-conditioned, the pews were cushioned and the singing was great. Did you notice people looking at me when I joined in with my deep baritone voice?"

"Yes, I noticed them," his wife responded. "But the next time we go to church, please try to sing 'Hallelujah, Hallelujah' and not 'Hialeah, Hialeah.'"
                    —*Complete Speaker's Galaxy of Funny Stories, Jokes and Anecdotes,* edited by WINSTON K. PENDLETON

An excited woman called her husband at work. "I won the lottery!" she exclaimed. "Pack your clothes!"

"Great!" he replied. "Summer or winter clothes?"

"All of them—I want you out of the house by six!"
                    —ASHLEY COOPER in Charleston, S.C., *News and Courier*

With a Rub of the Lamp

Experimenting with a trick, a magician accidentally changed his wife into a sofa and his two children into armchairs. He called an ambulance and they were rushed to the hospital. Later, the worried sorcerer phoned to check their condition.

"Resting comfortably," said the doctor.
                                        —*Today*

One day a man spotted a lamp by the roadside. He picked it up, rubbed it vigorously and a genie appeared.

"I'll grant you your fondest wish," the genie said.

The man thought for a moment, then said, "I want a spectacular job—a job that no man has ever succeeded at or has ever attempted to do."

"Poof!" said the genie. "You're a housewife."

—NICOLE BURKE

A despondent woman was walking along the beach when she saw a bottle on the sand. She picked it up and pulled out the cork. *Whoosh!* A big puff of smoke appeared.

"You have released me from my prison," the genie told her. "To show my thanks, I grant you three wishes. But take care, for with each wish, your mate will receive double of whatever you request."

"Why?" the woman asked. "That bum left me for another woman."

"That is how it is written," replied the genie.

The woman shrugged and then asked for a million dollars. There was a flash of light, and a million dollars appeared at her feet. At the same instant, in a far-off place, her wayward husband looked down to see twice that amount at his feet.

"And your second wish?"

"Genie, I want the world's most expensive diamond necklace." Another flash of light, and the woman was holding the precious treasure. And, in that distant place, her husband was looking for a gem broker to buy his latest bonanza.

"Genie, is it really true that my husband has two million dollars and more jewels than I do, and that he gets double of whatever I wish for?"

The genie said it was indeed true.

"Okay, genie, I'm ready for my last wish," the woman said. "Scare me half to death."

—TOM NEDWEK, quoted by ALEX THIEN
in the Milwaukee *Sentinel*

··

Overheard: "For some reason I didn't like that Disney movie. Aladdin rubbed me the wrong way."
—GARY APPLE in *Speaker's Idea File*

A man was trying to obtain a flat in Bombay. After many days of fruitless search he was returning to his slum home when he stopped to buy a tender coconut. But when he cut open the top of the coconut, smoke issued out and to the poor man's astonishment a huge genie materialized.

"Command and I will obey!" thundered the genie.

With awakening hope the man stuttered out, "I want a flat in Bombay."

"If I could get a flat for myself in Bombay," retorted the genie, "do you think I would have stayed inside a coconut?"
—RAJIV NAIR

Then there was the fellow who always had bad luck. Once he found a magic lamp, rubbed it, and a genie appeared and gave him the Midas touch. For the rest of his life, everything he touched turned into a muffler.
—*Orben's Comedy Fillers*

Arthur rubbed the old lamp he'd purchased at a flea market, and sure enough, a genie appeared. "Thanks for setting me free," said the grateful spirit.

"Aren't you going to grant me a wish?" asked Arthur.

"Are you kidding?" answered the genie. "If I could grant wishes, would I have been in that lousy lamp all this time?"
—STEVE KEUCHEL

"I thought you had the camera."

Travel

Up in the Air

It doesn't make sense," says comedian Elayne Boosler. "You're flying at 500 m.p.h., 30,000 feet in the air, and the pilot tells you to feel free to roam around the plane. But when you're on the ground taxiing to the gate at one m.p.h., he tells you to remain seated for your own safety."

Why is there mistletoe hanging over the baggage counter?" asked the airline passenger, amid the holiday rush.

The clerk replied, "It's so you can kiss your luggage good-bye."

—SEYMOUR ROSENBERG in the Spartanburg, S.C., *Herald-Journal*

A student-pilot was making his first helicopter flight. After the takeoff, the instructor explained the instruments and, pointing to the rotor blades, said, "That's the air conditioning."

The pupil looked at him in astonishment, and the instructor said, "You don't believe me, do you? Just wait until we reach 3,000 feet and I shut it off. Then you'll see what a hot spot this can be!"

—P. VAN WINKEL

An elderly woman was nervous about making her first flight in an airplane, so before takeoff she went to speak to the captain about her fears.

"You will bring me down safely, won't you?" she anxiously inquired.

"Don't worry, madam," was his friendly reply. "I haven't left anyone up there yet."

—COLLEEN BURGER

"I happen to be a frequent flyer, and this just doesn't feel right to me."

A jet ran into some turbulent weather. To keep the passengers calm, the flight attendants brought out the beverage carts.

"I'd like a soda," said a passenger in the first row. Moving along, the attendant asked the man behind her if he would like something.

"Yes, I would," he replied. "Give me whatever the pilot is drinking!"

—MARY J. MILLER

A small plane with an instructor and student on board hit the runway and bounced repeatedly until it came to a stop. The instructor turned to the student and said, "That was a very bad landing you just made."

"Me?" replied the student. "I thought *you* were landing."

—*The Cockle Bur*

The 747 was halfway across the Atlantic when the captain got on the loudspeaker: "Attention, passengers. We have lost one of our engines, but we can certainly reach London with the three we have left. Unfortunately, we will arrive an hour late as a result."

An hour later the captain made another announcement: "Sorry, but we lost another engine. Still, we can travel on two. I'm afraid we will now arrive two hours late."

Shortly thereafter, the passengers heard the captain's voice again: "Guess what, folks. We just lost our third engine, but please be assured we can fly with only one. We will now arrive in London three hours late."

At this point, one passenger became furious. "For Pete's sake," he shouted. "If we lose another engine, we'll be up here all night!"

—Nathaniel Scott Miller

At an airline ticket counter, a small boy, with his mother, told the agent he was two years old. The man looked at him suspiciously and asked, "Do you know what happens to little boys who lie?"

"Yes. They get to fly at half-price."

—Marlene Freedman in *Chevron USA*

Pilot to airline passengers: "Ladies and gentlemen, I have some good news and some bad news. The bad news is that we have a hijacker on board. The good news is, he wants to go to the French Riviera."

—*Parts Pups*

Q: What's a sure sign you're flying the wrong airline?

A: The pilot has a heart attack, and the air-traffic controller talks a flight attendant through takeoff.

—Peter S. Langston

The Concorde is great," says Howie Mandel. "Traveling at twice the speed of sound is fun—except you can't hear the movie till two hours after you land."

Two pilots were discussing the merits of a twin-engine, propeller-driven aircraft undergoing service trials. "How does it handle?" asked the pilot who hadn't yet flown the new plane.

"Oh, it's not bad," was the reply.

"How is it in asymmetric flight? One engine out?"

After thinking for a moment, the other pilot replied, "Ah, that's where it becomes tricky. If one engine quits, the other engine immediately takes you to the scene of the crash."

—Jim McCorkle

Wheeling

Lost on back roads in Vermont, a tourist collided with a local man at an intersection. He and the local got out to examine their bent fenders.

"Well, don't look like much," observed the local. "Whyn't we just take a little pull to steady our nerves." He grabbed a jug from his battered pickup, removed the stopper and handed it to the tourist.

After taking a good slug, the tourist handed the jug back to the local, who banged in the stopper and set the jug back in his truck.

"Aren't you going to have some?" asked the tourist.

The local shook his head. "Not till after the trooper comes."

—James Shannon

● ●

Anytime you see a young man open a car door for his girlfriend, either the car is new or the girlfriend is.

—ROBERT E. LIMBAUGH II in *Boys' Life*

A juggler, driving to his next performance, is stopped by the police. "What are those machetes doing in your car?" asks the cop.

"I juggle them in my act."

"Oh, yeah?" says the doubtful cop. "Let's see you do it." The juggler gets out and starts tossing and catching the knives. Another man driving by slows down to watch.

"Wow," says the passer-by. "I'm glad I quit drinking. Look at the test they're giving now!"

—NATALIE KAPLOWITZ

A young man was trying to park his car between two others. He put it in reverse, and *bang*—right into the car behind him. He then went forward and *bang*—right into the car in front.

A young woman watching the maneuver couldn't contain herself. "Do you always park by ear?" she asked.

—VENDERCI MARTINS VALENTE

A traffic cop pulled over a speeding motorist and asked, "Do you have any ID?"

The motorist replied, "About what?"

—MARTHA B. ROBERTS

After he finished his route, a bus driver had to explain to the supervisor why he was 10 minutes late: "I was stuck behind a big truck."

"But yesterday you were 10 minutes early," reminded the boss.

"Yeah," the bus driver replied. "But yesterday I was stuck behind a Porsche."

—TIM HARVEY

• •

Late for a return flight from Dublin, an American tourist in Ireland jumped into a cab. "Quick," he said, "get me to the airport as fast as you can!" The cabbie nodded and floored the gas pedal. Soon they were barreling along at more than 70 miles an hour.

Just ahead a stoplight was bright red. The cab shot through the intersection without slowing down in the slightest. "Are you blind?" shouted the tourist. "That was a red light!"

The cabbie was unfazed. "I don't believe in red lights, sir, nor do any of my five cab-driving brothers." After two more hair-raising hurtles through red lights, the tourist was relieved to see a green light. But right before the intersection, the cabbie slammed on the brakes. "Are you insane?" yelled the passenger. "That was a green light!"

"True, sir," replied the cabbie. "But you never know when one of my brothers may be coming through."

—E. H.

The truck driver stopped at a roadside diner. His waitress brought him a hamburger, a cup of coffee, and a piece of pie.

As the trucker was about to start eating, three men in leather jackets pulled up on motorcycles and came inside. One grabbed the man's hamburger, the second one drank his coffee and the other one took his pie. The truck driver didn't say a word. He got up, put on his jacket, paid the cashier and left.

One of the bikers said to the cashier, "Not much of a man, is he?"

"He's not much of a driver either," she replied. "He just ran his truck over three motorcycles."

—MICHAEL IAPOCE in *A Funny Thing Happened on the Way to the Boardroom*

Driving tip: If you rear-end a car on the freeway, your first move should be to hang up the phone.

—TOM ADAMS in *Comic Highlights*

"Fill'er up, sir?"

The driving instructor was giving lessons to an extremely nervous student who panicked whenever another car approached on a particular two-lane road. One day, however, they got to the same stretch of road, and she remained completely calm.

"This time you're doing fine!" exclaimed the instructor.

"Yes," the novice driver agreed. "Now when I see another car coming, I shut my eyes."

—M. HERBRINK

• •

Driving back from car-repair class, John said to his buddy, Joe, "I'm going to turn now. Could you stick your head out the window to see if the blinker's working?"

"Sure," Joe replied as he peeked outside. "It is, no it isn't, yes it is, no it isn't, yes it is . . . ."

—Paulo Cesar Menegusso

The young woman sat in her stalled car, waiting for help. Finally two men walked up to her.

"I'm out of gas," she purred. "Could you push me to a service station?"

They readily put their muscles to the car and rolled it several blocks. After a while, one looked up, exhausted, to see that they had just passed a filling station.

"How come you didn't turn in?" he yelled.

"I never go there," the woman shouted back. "They don't have full service."

—*Super Automotive Service*

What an automated society we live in. Have you ever noticed that when a traffic signal turns green, it automatically activates the horn of the car behind you?

—Robert Orben in *The American Legion Magazine*

Driving down a winding country road, a man came upon a youth running hard, three huge dogs snarling at his heels. The man screeched his car to a halt and threw open the door. "Get in, get in!" he shouted.

"Thanks," gasped the youth. "You're terrific. Most people won't offer a ride when they see I have three dogs!"

—P. A. Isaacson

Wife: "There's trouble with the car. It has water in the carburetor."

Husband: "Water in the carburetor? That's ridiculous."

Wife: "I tell you the car has water in the carburetor."

Husband: "You don't even know what a carburetor is. Where's the car?"

Wife: "In the swimming pool."

—*Executive Speechwriter Newsletter*

The villager on his first trip to the city was waiting at a bus stop one morning. After some hesitation he asked a woman, "Which bus should I take for Mahim?"

"Bus Number 177," the woman replied, and caught the next bus.

The same evening, the woman got off a bus at the same stop and found the villager still waiting. "Didn't you get the bus to Mahim?" she exclaimed.

"Not yet," he said wearily. "So far 168 buses have come and gone—eight more before mine arrives."

—C. P. MURGUDKAR

Did you hear about the director of the Department of Motor Vehicles who resigned on Tuesday?

He tried to resign on Monday, but found he'd been standing in the wrong line.

—DAVE MARGOLIS in *The Los Angeles Times*

You know it's time to get a new car when—

The traffic reporter on the radio begins to refer to you by name.

You make a *left* turn and your date falls out.

You lose the "stoplight challenge" to a 16-year-old on a moped.

—JAY TRACHMAN in *One to One*

"North face of Everest: howling winds, sub-zero cold, insufficient oxygen, menswear."

Explorations

One stupid guy reads an ad about a vacation cruise that costs only $100. After he signs up and pays, the travel agent hits him with a bat, knocks him unconscious, and throws him out the back door into the river. Soon another guy comes in, pays his fee, and gets the same treatment.

Fifteen minutes later, as the two are floating down the river together, the first man says, "I wonder if they're serving any food on this cruise."

"I don't know," the second guy replies. "They didn't last year."

—MEL SMITH in *The Los Angeles Times*

An Irish lad named Sean was doing so well with his furniture business that he decided to take a trip to France. When he returned to Ireland, his friend Brendan asked him, "Why did you go to France and you not speaking a word of the language? How could you make yourself understood?"

"Let me tell you," said Sean. "I met this lass in the park. I drew a picture of plates and food, and so we went out to eat. After drawing a picture of people dancing, we went to a nightclub. At midnight, could you imagine, she took my pen and drew a picture of a bed."

"Faith 'n' begorra!" exclaimed Brendan. "How did she know you were in the furniture business?"

—THOMAS R. McGUINNESS

Just before heading to Florida for spring break, a college student bought a skimpy bikini. She modeled it for her mother. "How do you like it?"

The parent stared in silence for a few moments, and then replied, "If I had worn a bathing suit like that when I was your age, you'd be four years older than you are right now."

—Quoted by JAMES DENT in Charleston, W. Va., *Gazette*

Two explorers, camped in the heart of the African jungle, were discussing their expedition. "I came here," said one, "because the urge to travel was in my blood. City life bored me, and the smell of exhaust fumes on the highways made me sick. I wanted to see the sun rise over new horizons and hear the flutter of birds that never had been seen by man. I wanted to leave my footprints on sand unmarked before I came. In short, I wanted to see nature in the raw. What about you?"

"I came," the second man replied, "because my son was taking saxophone lessons."

—AL BATT in *Capper's*

Heading into the jungle on his first safari, the American visitor was confident he could handle any emergency. He sidled up to the experienced native guide and said smugly, "I know that carrying a torch will keep lions away."

"True," the guide replied. "But it depends on how fast you carry the torch."

—E. H.

From a passenger ship one can see a bearded man on a small island who is shouting and desperately waving his hands.

"Who is it?" a passenger asks the captain.

"I've no idea. Every year when we pass, he goes mad."

—*Chayan*

One day, an explorer was captured by native warriors and taken to their chieftain, a gigantic man with teeth filed to dagger-like points. Desperately, the explorer tried to think of a way to save himself. He pulled out his cigarette lighter, held it in front of the chief's face and lit it, exclaiming, "Look! *Magic!*"

The chief's eyes were huge in astonishment. "It certainly must be magic," he said. "I have never seen a lighter light on the first try!"

—*Nuggets*

One hot, dry day in the West, a traveler arrived at a small highway café. Wiping the sweat from his brow, he turned to a deeply tanned old-timer sitting at the counter and asked, "When was the last time it rained here?"

The old man looked at him. "Son, you remember in the Bible when it says it rained for 40 days and 40 nights?"

"Well, yes, I sure do."

The old man continued, "We got an inch."

—DOUGLAS IRVING in *Arizona Highways*

● ●

On our railway, children age 10 and under travel at half-price. As the conductor began checking tickets, a woman sitting next to me told her daughter, "Now remember, you are only 10." The girl nodded her head.

The conductor approached and asked the girl, "How old are you?"

"Ten, sir."

"And when will you be 11?"

"When I get off this train!"

—THEODORUS HARI WAHUANTO

Two passengers on a ship are talking. "Can you swim?" asks one.

"No," says the other, "but I can shout for help in nine languages."

—MRS. ATTILANE NAGY

The sociologist on an African jungle expedition held up her camera to take pictures of the native children at play. Suddenly the youngsters began to yell in protest.

Turning red, the sociologist apologized to the chief for her insensitivity and told him she had forgotten that certain tribes believed a person lost his soul if his picture was taken. She explained to him, in long-winded detail, the operation of a camera. Several times the chief tried to get a word in, but to no avail.

Certain she had put all the chief's fears to rest, the sociologist then allowed him to speak. Smiling, he said, "The children were trying to tell you that you forgot to take off the lens cap!"

—SHARON SPENCE

"It's faster if you use the stairs inside."

"No, no, not a pride. It's a bunch of tourists."

Tourism Department

What's this daily charge for 'fruit'?" the hotel patron asked the manager. "We didn't eat any."

"But the fruit was placed in your room every day. It isn't our fault you didn't take advantage of it."

"I see," said the man as he subtracted $150 from the bill.

"What are you doing?" sputtered the manager.

"I'm subtracting 50 dollars a day for your kissing my wife."

"What? I didn't kiss your wife."

"Ah," replied the man, "but she was there."

—JAMES DENT in the Charleston, W. Va., *Gazette*

Travel agent: "I can get you three days and two nights in Rome for a hundred bucks."

Customer: "How come so cheap?"

Travel agent: "The days are July 11, 12 and 13. The nights are July 21 and 22."

—BRANT PARKER & JOHNNY HART, North America Syndicate

Asia was by far my favorite destination," the woman bragged at the party, though she had never been out of the United States. "Enigmatic and magical, beautiful beyond belief. And China, of course, is the pearl of the Asian oyster."

"What about the pagodas?" a man beside her asked. "Did you see them?"

"Did I *see* them? My dear, I had *dinner* with them."

—LORD-NELSON QUIST in *Playboy*

In a panic, a traveler called down to the hotel's front desk soon after checking in. "Help!" he yelled. "I'm trapped inside my room!"

"What do you mean, trapped?"

"Well, I see three doors," the man explained. "The first opens to a closet, and the second to a bathroom. And the third door has a 'Do Not Disturb' sign hanging on it."

—PETER S. GREENBERG, Los Angeles Times Syndicate

When the fellow called a motel and asked how much they charged for a room, the clerk told him that the rates depended on room size and number of people. "Do you take children?" the man asked.

"No, sir," replied the clerk. "Only cash and credit cards."

—*Successful Meetings Magazine*

"What do you say, honey? This looks like our kind of place."

An English traveler, asked by Australian immigration if he had a criminal record, expressed some surprise that such a qualification was still required.

—New Zealand *Herald*

A vacationer telephoned a seaside hotel to ask where it was. "It's only a stone's throw from the beach," he was told. "How will I recognize it?" asked the man. Back came the reply, "It's the one with all the broken windows."

—Bob Sterling

• •

A pair of honeymooners checked into the Watergate Hotel in Washington, D.C. That night, as the husband was about to turn off the light, his bride asked, "Do you think this room is bugged?"

"That was a long time ago, sweetheart," he reassured her.

"But what if there's a microphone somewhere? I'd be so embarrassed."

So the groom searched under tables and behind pictures. Then he turned back the rug. Sure enough, there was a funny-looking gizmo in the floor. He took out the screws, got rid of the hardware, and climbed into bed.

The next morning the newlyweds were awakened by a hotel clerk who wanted to know if they had slept well.

"We did," replied the groom. "Why do you ask?"

"It's rather unusual," the clerk answered. "Last night the couple in the room below yours had a chandelier fall on them."

—HENNY YOUNGMAN, quoted by ALEX THIEN in the Milwaukee
Sentinel

A New York retail clerk was suffering from aching feet. "It's all those years of standing," his doctor declared. "You need a vacation. Go to Miami, soak your feet in the ocean and you'll feel better."

When the man got to Florida, he went into a hardware store, bought two large buckets and headed for the beach. "How much for two buckets of that sea water?" he asked the lifeguard.

"A dollar a bucket," the fellow replied with a straight face.

The clerk paid him, filled his buckets, went to his hotel room and soaked his feet. They felt so much better he decided to repeat the treatment that afternoon. Again he handed the lifeguard two dollars. The young man took the money and said, "Help yourself."

The clerk started for the water, then stopped in amazement. The tide was out. "Wow," he said, turning to the lifeguard. "Some business you got here!"

—CARL D. KIRBY

A tourist was visiting New Mexico and was amazed at the dinosaur bones lying about.

"How old are these bones?" the tourist asked an elderly Native American, who served as a guide.

"Exactly one hundred million and three years old."

"How can you be so sure?" inquired the tourist.

"Well," replied the guide, "a geologist came by here and told me these bones were one hundred million years old, and that was exactly three years ago."

—ALLAN E. OSTAR

To celebrate their silver anniversary, a couple went to Niagara Falls and asked a motel clerk for a room. "We only have the honeymoon suite available," she told them.

"My wife and I've been married 25 years," the man said. "We don't need the honeymoon suite."

"Look, buddy," replied the clerk. "I might rent you Yankee Stadium, but you don't have to play baseball in it!"

—*Parts Pups*

An American couple visiting in a German village stepped into a small shop to look for souvenirs. The woman sneezed.

"*Gesundheit!*" said the clerk.

"Charles," said the American woman to her husband, "we're in luck. There's somebody here who speaks English."

—*Ohio Motorist*

At a swanky hotel, a guy walks up to the front desk and asks the clerk, "Do I register with you?"

"Not by any stretch of the imagination," snaps the woman.

—ASHLEY COOPER in the Charleston, S.C., *Post and Courier*

"His majesty the Kingpin!"

Public Domain

International Boundaries

Two highway workers are at a construction site when a car with diplomatic plates pulls up. "*Parlez-vous français?*" the driver asks. The two just stare.

"*Hablan ustedes español?*" the driver tries. They stare some more.

"*Sprechen Sie Deutsch?*" They continue to stare.

"*Parlate italiano?*" Nothing. Finally the man drives off in disgust.

One worker turns to the other and says, "Maybe we should learn a foreign language."

"What for?" the other replies. "That guy knew four of them, and a fat lot of good it did him."

—MAXIME COSMA, *The Best Jokes of Romania*

A minister was urged by his congregation to explain the difference between heaven and hell. "They're not as different as you might think," he said. "In heaven, the British are the policemen, the Germans are the mechanics, the Swiss run the trains, the French do the cooking, and the Italians are the lovers. In hell, only minor changes take place. The Germans are the policemen, the French are the mechanics, the Italians run the trains, the British do the cooking, and the Swiss are making love."

—JOHN MOLYNEUX in *The Bulletin*

Was Grandpa mad when they went through his luggage at the border?"

"Not in the least. They found his glasses that he'd lost two weeks earlier."

—MIKLOS MADARASZ

"In the interests of restoring calm to world trouble spots, UN peacekeepers invade Buckingham Palace."

The door label reads: UNITED NATIONS SECURITY COUNCIL (WRIST-SLAPPING DIVISION)

A near-sighted diplomat attended a ball at a South American embassy. When the orchestra struck up a tune, he felt he should start the dancing. Accordingly he walked over to a figure clad in red and said, "Beautiful lady in scarlet, would you do me the honor of waltzing with me?"

"Certainly not!" came the reply. "In the first place, this is not a waltz, but a tango. And in the second place, I am not a beautiful lady in scarlet. I'm the papal nuncio."

—ROBERT L. CLARKE, quoted by WILLIAM SAFIRE and
LEONARD SAFIR in *Leadership*

• •

Overheard: "The tragedy of Canada is that they had the opportunity to have French cuisine, British culture, and American technology, and instead they ended up with British cuisine, American culture, and French technology."

—WILL SHETTERLY

An Englishman awaiting the train to Paris at the station restaurant in Calais beckoned to the waiter and asked him in French laden with a heavy British accent, "Do you know the man smoking a pipe and reading a newspaper over by the heater?"

"No, sir. So many of our patrons are just passing through."

"Well, please call the manager for me then."

When the manager arrived, the Englishman repeated his question. The manager scrutinized the man by the heater.

"I'm sorry, sir, but I've never seen him before."

With that, the Englishman rose and walked over to the man. "Please accept my apologies, sir, for speaking to you without having been properly introduced," he said, "but your coat is on fire!"

—FRANÇOIS CHAUVIÈRE

There is a story that Soviet General Secretary Mikhail Gorbachev was late for a meeting and told his chauffeur to step on it. The chauffeur refused on the ground that it would be breaking the speeding laws. So Gorbachev ordered him into the back seat and got behind the wheel.

After a few miles, the car was stopped by a police patrol. The senior officer sent his subordinate to arrest the offender.

A moment later, the officer returned saying that the person was much too important to prosecute.

"Who is it?" demanded the police chief.

"I'm not sure, sir," replied the officer, "but Comrade Gorbachev is his chauffeur."

—"Observer" in *Financial Times*

A secret agent was sent to Ireland to pick up some sensitive information from an agent named Murphy. His instructions were to walk around town using a code phrase until he met his fellow agent.

He found himself on a desolate country road and finally ran into a farmer. "Hello," the agent said, "I'm looking for a man named Murphy."

"Well, you're in luck," said the farmer. "As it happens, there's a village right over the hill where the butcher is named Murphy, the baker is named Murphy, and three widows are named Murphy. Matter of fact, my name is Murphy."

Aha, the agent thought, here's my man. So he whispered the secret code: "The sun is shining...the grass is growing...the cows are ready for milking."

"Oh," said the farmer, "you're looking for Murphy the spy—he's in the village over in the other direction."

—RAYMOND W. SMITH in
Vital Speeches of the Day

On a visit to the United States, Gorbachev met a Russian who had immigrated to this country. "What do you do for a living here?" the Soviet leader asked him.

"My brother, my sister, and I work in a big factory."

"How do these capitalist bosses treat you?"

"Just fine," answered the man. "In fact, if you are walking home from work, the boss picks you up in his big car and drives you to your door. Another time, he treats you to a dinner in an expensive restaurant. Sometimes he takes you home for the weekend and buys you presents."

Gorbachev was stunned. "How often does this happen?"

"Well, to me, actually never. But to my sister, several times."

—Quoted by JAMES DENT in the
Charleston, W.Va., *Gazette*

Government at Its Biggest

A young man visited his local welfare office and was asked to give his surname—all other details would be on computer. The assistant typed in his name, then read from the screen: "You are James Herbert Roberts of Oldfield Lane, London, age 22; single; unemployed for one year; now working as a plumber for Jones & Co. It's all here, every last detail. Now, what is your query?"

"Well," said the man, "it's about the widow's pension you keep sending me."

—BILL NAYLOR

The president receives the news that his government is divided between optimists and pessimists. "Who are the optimists?" the president asks.

"They are those who believe that we will be eating grass by the end of the year," says the adviser.

"And the pessimists?"

"They are those who think that there won't be enough grass for everybody."

—*Veja*

Question: Why wasn't Rome built in a day?
Answer: Because it was a government job.
　　　　—GLENN E. SPRADLIN in the Louisville *Courier-Journal*

Why does the capital have so many one-way streets? So that all the civil servants coming in late won't collide with those going home early.

—ARNIE BENJAMIN, *The Daily News*

Man to friend: "I figured out why the Postal Service raised the postage rates. The extra four cents is for storage."

—ANGIE PAPADAKIS

You don't see me at Vegas or the track throwing my money around anymore," says Bob Hope. "I've got a government to support."

A veteran congressman was asked what he had learned in the rough-and-tumble of the political arena. "Well," he said, "I found it wasn't so much whether you won or lost, but how you placed the blame."

—*American Agriculturalist Magazine*

At a Washington cocktail party, two strangers struck up a conversation. After a few minutes of small talk, one said, "Have you heard the latest White House joke?"

The second fellow held up his hand. "Wait, before you begin, I should tell you that I work in the White House."

"Oh, don't worry," the first man replied. "I'll tell it very slowly."

—T. J. MCINERNEY in *Globe*

Overheard at the Food and Drug Administration: "If laughter is the best medicine, shouldn't we be *regulating* it?"

—BALOO in *The Wall Street Journal*

Highway sign: "SPEED LIMIT 65 for most cars and some trucks under 8,000 pounds—only if they're empty, unless you weigh over 300 pounds—then divide by six. For additional information call the IRS, which helped write this."

—MIKE PETERS, Tribune Media Services

"Ladies and gentlemen, I believe I can announce that at long last we've isolated the gene that determines political affiliation."

Four friends met at a restaurant for lunch. For quite a while, no one said a word. Finally the first man mumbled, "Oh, boy!" To which the next one said, "It's awful." The third then muttered, "What are ya gonna do?"

"Listen," exclaimed the last friend, "if you guys don't stop talking politics, I'm leaving!"

—*The Big Book of Jewish Humor,* edited by
WILLIAM NOVAK and MOSHE WALDOKS

It's a Crime

Did you hear about the desperado who tried to hijack a bus full of Japanese tourists? Fortunately, police had 5,000 photographs of the suspect.

—BARRY CRYER on *American Radio Theater*

Can you describe your assailant?" asked the officer as he helped the bruised and battered man get up.

"Sure," the man replied. "That's what I was doing when he hit me."

—ALAN THOMAS in *Quote*

A man was applying for a job as a prison guard. The warden said, "Now these are real tough guys in here. Do you think you can handle it?"

"No problem," the applicant replied. "If they don't behave, out they go!"

—JOEY ADAMS

When a Colorado mine operator found that his office safe had jammed, he called the nearby state prison and asked whether any of the inmates might know how to open it. Soon, a convict and a prison guard showed up at the office. The inmate spun the dials, listened intently and calmly opened the safe door.

"I'm much obliged," said the mine operator. "How much do you figure I owe you?"

"Well," said the prisoner, "the last time I opened a safe I got $25,000."

—W. T. LITTLE

•••

Two prisoners were making their escape over the jailhouse roof when one of them dislodged a tile. "Who's there?" shouted a guard.

The first prisoner replied with a convincing imitation of a cat's meow. Reassured, the guard went back to his rounds.

But then the second prisoner dislodged another tile. The guard repeated, "Who's there?"

"The other cat," answered the prisoner.

—LAURENT GREBERT

Sent to prison as a first offender, a student of English was told by a longtime inmate that if he made amorous advances to the warden's wife, she'd get him released quickly.

"But I can't do that," he protested. "It's wrong to end a sentence with a proposition."

—*Financial Times*

Comedy writer Paul Ryan tells of the cable TV repairman who was charged with faking his own kidnapping. Police became suspicious when they had to wait at home with the ransom from 9 AM to 5 PM.

—*The Los Angeles Times*

Outside city hall, a boy selling newspapers bellowed, "Extra! Extra! Read all about it! Two men swindled!" A man walked up to the boy, bought a paper, and sat down to read it. "Hey, kid," he protested a few moments later, "there's nothing in here about two men being cheated."

"Extra! Extra!" shouted the boy. "Three men swindled!"

—MIKE LESSITER in *Country Chuckles,*
Cracks & Knee-Slappers

"Mr. Cosgrove has stepped away from his desk.
May I take a message?"

Three friends who always argued about who was the smartest are sitting on death row. The first one's number comes up, but when he sits down in the electric chair, nothing happens. The warden commutes his sentence on the spot and releases him.

Same thing happens with the second friend and he's let go. Then the third guy steps up to the platform and sits down.

The switch is pulled and again there's no charge. But before the warden can say anything, the prisoner starts pointing excitedly. "You know," he says, "if you'd just cross that black wire with the yellow one. . . . "

—Quoted on *The Gary McKee Hometown Radio Show*,
WSB-AM, Atlanta

People say New Yorkers can't get along. Not true. I saw two New Yorkers, complete strangers, sharing a cab. One guy took the tires and the radio; the other guy took the engine.

—*Late Show with David Letterman*

The inmate was aware that all prison mail passes through censors. When he got a letter from his wife asking about the family garden—"Honey, when do I plant potatoes?"—he wrote back, "Do not, under any circumstances, dig up our old garden spot. That's where I buried all my guns."

Within days his wife wrote back, "Six investigators came to the house. They dug up every square inch of the back yard."

By return mail she got his answer: "Now is the time to plant potatoes."

—REV. ROBERT MOORE JR., quoted by CHARLES ALLBRIGHT in
the *Arkansas Democrat Gazette*

Higher Education

During a college examination, the professor found a student peeking at a classmate's answers.

"How can you cheat so blatantly?" the professor shouted. "You have already stolen more than one look at your classmate's paper!"

"Don't blame me, sir," replied the student. "If his handwriting weren't so bad, I could have got it all at one glance."

—SHIH YU HSIEH

Q: What's the difference between ignorance and apathy?
A: I don't know and I don't care.

—*Daily Telegraph*

A young man hired by a supermarket reported for his first day of work. The manager greeted him with a warm handshake and a smile, gave him a broom and said, "Your first job will be to sweep out the store."

"But I'm a college graduate," the young man replied indignantly.

"Oh, I'm sorry. I didn't know that," said the manager. "Here, give me the broom—I'll show you how."

—RICHARD L. WEAVER II in *Vital Speeches of the Day*

During a lecture for medical students, the professor listed as the two best qualities of a doctor the ability to conquer revulsion and the need for keen powers of observation. He illustrated this by stirring a messy substance with his finger and then licking his finger clean. Then he called a student to the front and made him do the same.

Afterward the professor remarked, "You conquered your revulsion, but your powers of observation are not very good. I stirred with my forefinger, but I licked my middle finger."

—S.K.D.

Our son came home from college for the weekend and I asked him, "How are things going?"

He said, "Good."

I said, "And the dormitory?"

He said, "Good."

I said, "They've always had a strong football team. How do you think they'll do this year?"

He said, "Good."

I said, "Have you decided on your major yet?"

He said, "Yes."

I said, "What is it?"

He said, "Communications."

—*Orben's Current Comedy*

"Is this any way to treat a dissident?"

Our economics professor talks to himself. Does yours?"
"Yes, but he doesn't realize it. He thinks we're listening!"
—CHARISMA B. RAMOS

During class, the chemistry professor was demonstrating the properties of various acids. "Now I'm dropping this silver coin into this glass of acid. Will it dissolve?"

"No, sir," a student called out.

"No?" queried the professor. "Perhaps you can explain why the silver coin won't dissolve."

"Because if it would, you wouldn't have dropped it in."
—HERBERT V. PROCHNOW, *Speaker's and Toastmaster's Handbook*

I'd like to donate a million dollars, tax-free, to this institution," a Texan announced to the president of a small college. "But there's a condition. I would like an honorary degree for my horse."

"Horse?" stammered the president.

"Yes, for my mare, Betsy. She's carried me faithfully for many years, and I think she deserves a doctorate in transportation."

"But we can't give a degree to a horse!"

"Sorry, then you don't get the million dollars."

The board of trustees was hastily convened and each member in turn condemned the idea as a disgrace. Finally the oldest trustee spoke. "Let's take the money," he said. "It's about time we gave a degree to a *whole* horse!"

—Isaac Asimov, *Asimov Laughs Again*

An engineer, a mathematician, and a physicist were standing around the university flagpole when an English professor wandered by. "What are you doing?" he asked.

"We need to know the height of the flagpole," answered one, "and we're discussing the formulas we might use to calculate it."

"Watch!" said the English professor. He pulled the pole from its fitting, laid it on the grass, borrowed a tape measure and said, "Exactly 24 feet." Then he replaced the pole and walked away.

"English professor!" sneered the mathematician. "We ask him for the height, and he gives us the length."

—*The Jokesmith*

"We super-rich are few in number. People should value us instead of always picking on us!"

Money Matters

The Rich and the Foolish

A tightwad was convinced by a friend to buy a couple of tickets in the state lottery. But after he won the big prize, he didn't seem happy. "What's wrong?" the friend asked. "You just became a millionaire!"

"I know," he groaned. "But I can't imagine why I bought that second ticket!"

—Ohio Motorist

A stockbroker had made millions of dollars for an Arabian oil sheik. The sheik was so pleased he offered her rubies, gold, and a silver-plated Rolls-Royce. She declined the gifts, telling him she had merely done her job. But the sheik insisted.

"Well," the woman said, "I've recently taken up golf. A set of golf clubs would be a fine gift."

Weeks went by. One morning the stockbroker received a letter from him.

"So far I have bought you three golf clubs," it said, "but I hope you will not be disappointed because only two of them have swimming pools."

*—*ALEX THIEN *in the Milwaukee* Sentinel

Selling at an auction was halted when the auctioneer announced, "Someone in the room has just lost his wallet containing $1,000. He is offering a reward of $250 for its immediate return." After a moment of silence, there was a call from the back of the room, "$255."

—Rotary Down Under

An MG Midget pulled alongside a Rolls-Royce at a traffic light. "Do you have a car phone?" its driver asked the guy in the Rolls.

"Of course I do," replied the haughty deluxe-car driver.

"Well, do you have a fax machine?"

The driver in the Rolls sighed. "I have that too."

"Then do you have a double bed in the back?" the Midget driver wanted to know.

Ashen-faced, the Rolls driver sped off. That afternoon, he had a mechanic install a double bed in his auto.

A week later, the Rolls driver passes the same MG Midget, which is parked on the side of the road—back windows fogged up and steam pouring out. The arrogant driver pulls over, gets out of the Rolls and bangs on the Midget's back window until the driver sticks his head out. "I want you to know that I had a double bed installed," brags the Rolls driver.

The Midget driver is unimpressed. "You got me out of the shower to tell me that?"

—Quoted by DAVID GREASON, New York Times News Service

A 70-year-old millionaire had just married a beautiful 20-year-old.

"You crafty old codger," said his friend. "How did you get such a lovely young wife?"

"Easy," the millionaire replied. "I told her I was 95."

—FIONA GOLDING

The miserly millionaire called a family conference. "I'm placing a box of money in the attic," he said. "When I die, I intend to grab it on my way up to heaven. See to it that no one touches it until it's my time to go."

The family respected his wishes. After his death the millionaire's wife looked in the attic. The box was still there. "The fool!" she said. "I *told* him he should have put it in the basement."

—GENE JENNINGS

A yuppie was driving his new BMW convertible. He had the top down, his right hand on the wheel, and his left arm hanging over the door. With the tape deck going full blast, he didn't notice the rust bucket that pulled around to pass until it sideswiped him. The yuppie pulled to a stop.

"My car!" he cried. "My beautiful car!"

When a policeman came by, the yuppie told him about the accident. His car was a wreck, and it didn't even have 50 miles on it.

"You've got more to worry about than your car," the officer replied. "You need an ambulance. Your arm is badly injured."

The yuppie looked at his arm and cried, "My Rolex watch—my beautiful Rolex!"

—ALEX THIEN in the Milwaukee *Sentinel*

When the preacher's car broke down on a country road, he walked to a nearby roadhouse to use the phone. After calling for a tow truck, he spotted his old friend, Frank, drunk and shabbily dressed at the bar. "What happened to you, Frank?" asked the good reverend. "You used to be rich."

Frank told a sad tale of bad investments that had led to his downfall. "Go home," the preacher said. "Open your Bible at random, stick your finger on the page and there will be God's answer."

Some time later, the preacher bumped into Frank, who was wearing Gucci shoes, sporting a Rolex watch, and had just stepped out of a Mercedes. "Frank," said the preacher, "I am glad to see things really turned around for you."

"Yes, preacher, and I owe it all to you," said Frank. "I opened my Bible, put my finger down on the page and there was the answer—Chapter 11."

—PATRICK DIXON

"I don't think you're trying very hard to look at things from a royal perspective."

And then there's the shop-a-holic whose friend complimented her on her new car. "Oh, thanks," the woman replied. "I'm getting about 20 malls per gallon!"

—*Nuggets*

Only the billionaire and his friend remained after all the guests at his weekend ranch party scurried off for the afternoon's entertainment. The host answered the phone and slammed down the receiver in disgust. "I have to go to Dallas, and I've no way to get there!"

"Sure you do," his friend reassured him. "Isn't that a Cadillac convertible with the keys in it?"

"Yes, but that's my wife's car."

"So why can't you use it?"

"Are you kidding? The windshield's ground to her prescription."

—David Cox

Having purchased a new car, my friend was chary of hiring a new chauffeur because he had been warned that most chauffeurs exchanged new car parts for old and made some money on the sly. However, since my friend did not know how to drive, he had to engage a chauffeur, but he questioned every movement of the driver.

Once when we were riding together, the car slowed, then picked up speed.

"What happened?" my friend asked the driver.

"I just changed the gear, sir," the driver replied.

Turning to me, my friend whispered, "I have to fire this fellow. He not only changed the gear but has the audacity to admit it!"

—M. L. Bhagat

A guy walks up to the owner of a store and says, "You probably don't remember me, but about five years ago I was broke. I came in here and asked you for $10, and you gave it to me."

The store owner smiles and replies, "Yes, I remember."

The guy says, "Are you still game?"

—Ron Dentinger in the Dodgeville, Wis., *Chronicle*

A farmer who was notoriously miserly called a doctor to attend his sick wife.

"They say you're a skinflint," said the doctor. "Can I be sure of my fee?"

"Whether you kill my wife or cure her, you'll get your money without having to sue," said the farmer.

But the woman died, despite all the doctor's efforts to save her. He duly asked for his payment.

"Did you cure my wife?" asked the man.

"No," admitted the doctor.

"Did you kill her?"

"Certainly not!" the doctor said indignantly.

"Well, then, I owe you nothing."

—MICHELE VACQUIER

Mrs. Flinders decided to have her portrait painted. She told the artist, "Paint me with diamond earrings, a diamond necklace, emerald bracelets, and a ruby pendant."

"But you're not wearing any of those things."

"I know," said Mrs. Flinders. "It's in case I should die before my husband. I'm sure he'd remarry right away, and I want her to go nuts looking for the jewelry."

—MAE MORRISON

Take a pencil and paper," the teacher said, "and write an essay with the title 'If I Were a Millionaire.' "

Everyone but Philip, who leaned back with arms folded, began to write furiously.

"What's the matter," the teacher asked. "Why don't you begin?"

"I'm waiting for my secretary," he replied.

—BERNADETTE NAGY

"I like to think of myself as an artist, and money is the medium in which I work best."

High Finance

Houston stockbroker to client: "If you put one hundred thousand dollars in a certificate of deposit at the bank, you get either a toaster or an offshore drilling rig. But hurry. The toasters are going fast."
—BILL SHEPHERD, quoted by PAUL HARASIM
in the Houston *Post*

Chicken Little on Wall Street: "The sky is making a technical correction!"

—*Current Comedy*

A pair of economists went to a restaurant for lunch. "Never mind the food," one said to the waitress. "Just bring us the bill so we can argue about it."

—CAROL SIMPSON in *Funny Times*

I'm thinking of leaving my husband," complained the economist's wife. "All he ever does is stand at the end of the bed and tell me how good things are going to be."

—JAY TRACHMAN in *One to One*

The sales manager was complaining to a colleague about one of his salesmen. "George is so forgetful that it's a wonder he can sell anything. I asked him to pick up some sandwiches on his way back from lunch, but I'm not sure he'll even remember to come back."

Just then, the door flew open and in came George. "You'll never guess what happened!" he shouted. "At lunch, I met Fred Brown, the president of a Fortune 500 company. He hadn't bought anything from us in 10 years. Well, we got to talking, and he gave me an order worth 15 million dollars!"

"See?" said the sales manager. "I told you he'd forget the sandwiches."

—*Executive Speechwriter Newsletter*

The economy is weird," remarked one worker to another. "My bank failed before the toaster did."

—*Coffee Break*

"A monster called the commodities market tried to eat me today."

A bank in New York City is now making it possible to buy and sell stock using their ATM machines. This is great—it gives muggers a chance to diversify their portfolios.

—*Late Show with David Letterman*

A man was forever writing to his bank asking for his overdraft limit to be increased. The bank had always obliged, but when things eventually started to get critical, he received a letter from the manager that began: "Dear Sir. We are concerned about three overdrawn accounts at this bank, your own, Mexico's and Brazil's—in that order."

—VINCENT MURPHY

Question: What do you need to make a small fortune on Wall Street?

Answer: A large fortune.

—Country

Overheard: "Things are still bad in the banking industry. The other day, a friend of mine went to the bank and asked the teller to check her balance. The guy leaned over and pushed her!"

—TOM BLAIR in the San Diego *Union-Tribune*

A woman visited the bank to close her account because she was convinced the institution was going under.

Asked by a startled manager why she thought so, she produced one of her checks, endorsed by the bank, "Insufficient funds."

—Financial Mail

Loan Officer: "Based on your credit history, it seems the only kind of loan you qualify for is an auto loan."

Customer: "You mean money to buy a car?"

Loan Officer: "I mean money you lend yourself."

—J. C. DUFFY, Universal Press Syndicate

At a testimonial dinner in his honor, a wealthy businessman gave an emotional speech. "When I came to this city 50 years ago," he said, "I had no car, my only suit was on my back, the soles of my shoes were thin, and I carried all my possessions in a paper bag."

After dinner, a young man nervously approached. "Sir, I really admire your accomplishments. Tell me, after all these years, do you still remember what you carried in that brown paper bag?"

"Sure, son," he said. "I had $300,000 in cash and $500,000 in negotiable securities."

—The Lion

T. Boone Pickens told this joke to a group of bankers:

A banker calls in an oilman to review his loans. "We loaned you a million to revive your old wells, and they went dry," says the banker.

"Coulda been worse," the oilman replies.

"Then we loaned you a million to drill new wells, and they were dry."

"Coulda been worse."

"Then we loaned you another million for new drilling equipment, and it broke down."

"Coulda been worse."

"I'm getting tired of hearing that!" snaps the banker. "How could it have been worse?"

"Coulda been *my* money," says the oilman.

An accountant answered an advertisement for a top job with a large firm. At the end of the interview, the chairman said, "One last question—what is three times seven?"

The accountant thought for a moment and replied, "Twenty-two."

Outside he checked himself on his calculator and concluded he had lost the job. But two weeks later he was offered the post. He asked the chairman why he had been appointed when he had given the wrong answer.

"You were the closest," the chairman replied.

—S. NETTLE

I think my wages are frozen," one worker said to another. "When I opened my pay envelope, a little light went on."

—ROGER DEVLIN in the Tulsa *Tribune*

Answer: Rugs, fish batter, and savings and loan executives.

Question: List three things that should be beaten every Friday.

—JOHNNY CARSON on *The Tonight Show*

Edith and Norbert had a knock-down, drag-out battle over his inability to earn a better living. She told him he wasn't forceful enough in asking the boss for a raise.

"Tell him," she yelled, "that you have seven children. You also have a sick mother, you have to sit up many nights, and you have to clean the house because you can't afford a maid."

Several days later, Norbert came home from work, stood before his wife and calmly announced that the boss had fired him. "Why?" asked Edith.

"He says I have too many outside activities."

—The Larry Wilde Treasury of Laughter

Dialogue between a sharp-tongued boss and a dissatisfied employee seeking a raise: "I know perfectly well you aren't being paid what you're worth!"

"So . . ." asked the employee, his hope returning.

"But I can't allow you to starve to death, can I?"

—MADAME B. LEGÉ

Buyers Beware

Said a skeptical customer to a used-car dealer: "And how is your customer service?"

"Oh, that's first class. Anybody who buys a car from us gets a free copy of the latest railroad train schedules!"

—Der Stern

Sign in store window: "Any faulty merchandise will be cheerfully replaced with merchandise of equal quality."

—MARTHA JANE B. CATLETT

In Jaipur, India, a man broke his own world record for tiny writing. He squeezed 1,314 characters onto a single grain of rice. When he finished, he went back to his old job of printing rental-car contracts.

—JOHNNY CARSON on *The Tonight Show*

Husband, holding mail-order catalog, to wife: "It says on the cover that if we don't buy $10 worth of merchandise, they'll send our name to every catalog in the country!"

—SCHOCHET in *The Wall Street Journal*

When he found a six-year-old shoe-repair ticket in the pocket of an old suit, Brown called the shop to see if the shoes were still around.

"Were they black wingtips needing half soles?" asked a clerk.

"Yes," said Brown.

"We'll have them ready in a week."

—Quoted in *Lutheran Digest*

An optometrist was instructing a new employee on how to charge a customer. "As you are fitting his glasses, if he asks how much they cost, say '$75.' If his eyes don't flutter, say 'For the frames. The lenses will be $50.' If his eyes still don't flutter, you add 'Each.' "

—MAMIE BROWN

A gentleman entered a busy florist shop that displayed a large sign that read "Say It with Flowers."

"Wrap up one rose," he told the florist.

"Only one?" the florist asked.

"Just one," the customer replied. "I'm a man of few words."

—*Domenica del Corriere*

"You call that the trappings of wealth?"

Overheard: "I think our bank is in trouble. I was about to complete a withdrawal at the ATM and the machine asked me if I wanted to go double or nothing."

—*The Rotarian*

These yuppies are really getting to me," a man complained to his friend. "Have you seen the new funeral home in New York? It's called 'Death 'n' Things.' "

—JIM KERR, WWPR, New York

I think it's wrong," says comedian Steven Wright, "that only one company makes the game Monopoly."

I went to a bookstore today," says comic Brian Kiley, "and I asked the manager where the self-help section was. She said, 'If I told you, that would defeat the whole purpose.'"

I can't believe what's happened to gas prices! The other day I handed the kid at the pump a $20 bill, and he used it to wipe the dipstick!

—Quoted by PETE SUMMERS, WLAD, Danbury, Conn.

As the cashier totaled the man's purchases, she asked, "Do you wish to charge?"

Looking at the amount, he answered, "No. I think I'll surrender."

—GEORGE E. BERGMAN

If It Isn't Death, It's Taxes

Once, a man with an alligator walked into a pub and asked the bartender, "Do you serve IRS agents here?"

"Sure do," the barkeep replied.

"Good, give me a beer," said the man. "And my gator'll have an IRS agent."

—*Farmer's Digest*

Discussing the environment with his friend, one man asked, "Which of our natural resources do you think will become exhausted first?"

"The taxpayer," answered the other.

—WINSTON K. PENDLETON, *Complete Speaker's Galaxy of Funny Stories, Jokes and Anecdotes*

Two IRS agents were traveling through a rural area when their car broke down. They walked to a nearby mansion and knocked on the door. A beautiful widow answered and said they were welcome to spend the night while her hired hands worked on the car.

Months later one of the agents received a package of legal documents. After surveying the contents, he quickly called the other agent.

"When we were up in the country," the first agent asked, "did you slip away in the night and go to that widow's bedroom?"

"Yes," the second agent admitted.

"Did you use my name?"

"Why, yes, but how'd you find out?"

"She died and left me her estate."

—GAYLEN K. BUNKER

A grieving widow was discussing her late husband with a friend. "My Albert was such a good man, and I miss him so. He provided well for me with that fifty-thousand-dollar insurance policy—but I would give a thousand of it just to have him back."

—*Farmer's Digest*

Mrs. Willencot was very frugal. When her husband died, she asked the newspaper how much it would cost for a death notice.

"Two dollars for five words."

"Can I pay for just two words?" she asked. "Willencot dead."

"No, two dollars is the minimum. You still have three words."

Mrs. Willencot thought a moment. "Cadillac for sale."

—PATRICIA SCHULTZ

My tax man is so considerate and compassionate," says Joey Adams. "He's the only accountant I know with a recovery room."

"Look, I know it's not fair, but taking everyone at the flat age of 37 greatly simplifies the system."

On her eightieth birthday, a woman from Brooklyn decides to prepare her last will and testament. She goes to her rabbi to make two final requests. First, she insists on cremation.

"What is your second request?" the rabbi asks.

"I want my ashes scattered over Bloomingdale's."

"Why Bloomingdale's?"

"Then I'll be sure that my daughters visit me twice a week."

—*The Big Book of Jewish Humor,* edited by
WILLIAM NOVAK and MOSHE WALDOKS

The couple had reached an age where the wife thought it was time to start considering wills and funeral arrangements rather than be caught unprepared. Her husband, however, wasn't too interested in the topic. "Would you rather be buried or cremated?" she asked him.

There was a pause, then he replied from behind his paper, "Surprise me."

—JIM GIBSON in the Victoria, B.C., *Times-Colonist*

A guy walked into the tax collector's office with a huge bandage on his nose. "Had an accident?" asked the tax agent.

"No," answered the man. "I've been paying through it for so long, it gave way under the strain."

—RALPH GOLDSMITH in the Boscobel, Wis., *Dial*

Fire swept the plains and burned down the farmer's barn. While he surveyed the wreckage, his wife called their insurance company and asked them to send a check for $50,000, the amount of insurance on the barn.

"We don't give you the money," a company official explained. "We replace the barn and all the equipment in it."

"In that case," replied the wife, "cancel the policy I have on my husband."

—NAOMI WILKINS in *Woman's World*

President Clinton says he looks forward to the day a citizen can call the IRS and get the right answer to a question," says Jay Leno. "I look forward to the day I can call the IRS and get a voice that says, 'Sorry, that number has been disconnected.'"

"I suppose it's inevitable that we occasionally lose someone to a better mousetrap!"

Technology

Gadgets and Gizmos

Frank was setting up a sundial in his yard when a neighbor asked, "What's that for?"

Frank stopped to explain, "The sun hits that small triangular spike and casts a shadow on the face of the sundial. Then, as the sun moves across the sky, the shadow also moves across the calibrated dial, enabling a person to determine the correct time."

The neighbor shook his head. "What will they think of next?"

—RON DENTINGER in the
Dodgeville, Wis., *Chronicle*

Son to his father as they watch television: "Dad, tell me again how when you were a kid you had to walk all the way across the room to change the channel."

—BUCELLA in *VFW*

Overheard: "I hate talking cars. A voice out of nowhere says things like, 'Your door is ajar.' Why don't they say something really useful, like 'There's a state trooper hiding behind that bush.' "

—*Current Comedy*

And then there's the fellow who's sorry he ever installed a car telephone. He finds it such a nuisance having to run to the garage every time it rings.

—*The Rotarian*

One hypochondriac to another: "My doctor is on the cutting edge of technology. He told me to take two aspirin and fax him in the morning."

—*Current Comedy*

LONG-RANGE LASER SURGERY

Dragnet's Sgt. Joe Friday decided to upgrade the office communication system, so he went to an electronics store to see what was available. A saleswoman showed Friday the latest in cellular phones, intercoms, facsimile machines, and two-way radios. "Are you interested in purchasing a new telephone system?" she asked.

"No," replied Friday. "Just the fax, ma'am."

—TIM MOORE

Clem decided it was time to purchase a new saw to help clear his heavily timbered property. A salesman showed him the latest model chain saw and assured him that he could easily cut three or four cords of wood per day with it.

But the first day Clem barely cut one cord of wood. The second morning he arose an hour earlier and managed to cut a little over one cord. The third day he got up even earlier but only managed to achieve a total of 1 1/2 cords of wood.

Clem returned the saw to the store the next day and explained the situation. "Well," said the salesman, "let's see what's the matter." He then pulled the cable and the chain saw sprang into action.

Leaping back, Clem exclaimed, "What the heck is that noise?"

—GREGORY POTTER

Overheard: "Even my mother is getting caught up in our high-tech environment. Just the other day she was complaining, 'You don't write, you don't call, you don't fax.'"

—*Current Comedy for Speakers*

Did you hear about the high-tech ventriloquist?
He can throw his voice mail.

—GARY APPLE in *Speaker's Idea File*

And what would you like for Christmas this year?" a department store Santa asked the cute kid sitting on his lap.

The little girl was indignant. "Didn't you get the fax I sent you?"

—Quoted by ELSTON BROOKS in the Fort Worth *Star-Telegram*

There's a new telephone service that lets you test your IQ over the phone," says Jay Leno. "It costs $3.95 a minute. If you make the call at all, you're a moron. If you're on the line for three minutes, you're a complete idiot."

Overheard: "Yesterday I got my tie stuck in the fax machine. Next thing I knew, I was in Los Angeles."

—STEVE HAUPT

When I was a youngster," complained the frustrated father, "I was disciplined by being sent to my room without supper. But my son has his own color TV, phone, computer, and CD player."

"So what do you do?" asked his friend.

"I send him to *my* room!"

—*Capper's*

They say by the year 2000, video cameras will be the size of postage stamps and will cost 50 dollars. Of course by then postage stamps will cost 60 dollars . . . .

—WAYNE COTTER, *Comic Strip Live*, Fox TV

Satan agreed to be interviewed on the Larry King show. Asked what he thought were his greatest accomplishments, the devil thought for a minute.

"I always look back with a smile on the sinking of the *Titanic*," he mused. "But there are so many fond memories of wars, disasters, and cities laid waste, it's hard to pick out a favorite."

"Come on," pressed King. "There must be one foul deed you consider your crowning achievement."

"Well, yes," admitted Satan. "I invented Call Waiting."

—ARGUS HAMILTON in Oklahoma City *Daily Oklahoman*

My sister gave birth in a state-of-the-art delivery room," said one man to another. "It was so high-tech that the baby came out cordless."

—*Current Comedy*

VIRTUAL CEO

Department store automatic answering machine:

"If you are calling to order or send money, press 5.

"If you are calling to register a complaint, press 6 4 5 9 8 3 4 8 2 2 9 5 5 3 9 2.

"Have a good day."

—HAL THUROW

Patron: "What time do you have?"

Bartender: "I don't have a watch anymore. I bought one that was waterproof, dustproof, and shockproof."

Patron: "Well, where is it?"

Bartender: "It caught fire."

—YOUNG and DRAKE, King Features Syndicate

Phone-answering machines for the rich and famous:
•Sylvester Stallone—"Yo. You. Message. Now."
•Sally Field—"If you like me—if you really *like* me—leave your name and number after the beep."
•Clint Eastwood—"Go ahead, leave a message. Make my day."
•Shirley MacLaine—"I already know who you are and what you're calling about. Simply leave a brief description of your present incarnation."

—MAUREEN LARKIN in *Ladies' Home Journal*

Did you hear about the robot that was so ugly it had a face only a motor could love?

—SHELBY FRIEDMAN

Two executives in expensive suits stopped off at a small country bar. As the bartender served them, he heard a muffled *beep beep* sound and watched as one of the men calmly removed a pen from his inside coat pocket and began carrying on a conversation. When he was done talking, the exec noticed the bartender and other customers giving him puzzled looks. "I was just answering a call on my state-of-the-art cellular pen," he explained.

A short while later another odd tone was heard. This time the second executive picked up his fancy hat, fiddled with the lining and started talking into it. After a few minutes he put the hat back on the bar. "That was just a call on my state-of-the-art cellular hat," he said matter-of-factly.

A few stools down one of the locals suddenly let out a loud burp. "Quick!" he exclaimed. "Anybody got a piece of paper? I have a fax comin' in!"

—*John Boy & Billy,* Radio Network

While Milgrom waited at the airport to board his plane, he noticed a computer scale that would give your weight and a fortune. He dropped a quarter in the slot, and the computer screen displayed: "You weigh 195 pounds, you're married, and you're on your way to San Diego." Milgrom stood there dumbfounded.

Another man put in a quarter and the computer read: "You weigh 184 pounds, you're divorced, and you're on your way to Chicago."

Milgrom said to the man, "Are you divorced and on your way to Chicago?"

"Yes," came the reply.

Milgrom was amazed. Then he rushed to the men's room, changed his clothes and put on dark glasses. He went to the machine again. The computer read: "You still weigh 195 pounds, you're still married, and you just missed your plane to San Diego!"

—STEVE WOZNIAK and LARRY WILDE,
The Official Computer Freaks Joke Book

Bright Ideas

Q: How many car salesmen does it take to change a light bulb?
A: I'm just going to work this out on my calculator, and I think you're going to be pleasantly surprised.

—ROBERT WILBURN, quoted by
MARY ANN MADDEN in *New York*

How many politicians does it take to change a light bulb?
A. Five—one to change it and four to deny it.

—TINA FRENCH

Q: How many bullies does it take to change a light bulb?
A: Four. Do you have a problem with that?

—DENNIS LEEKE

Q: "How many bureaucrats does it take to change a light bulb?"

A: "Two. One to assure us that everything possible is being done while the other screws the bulb into a water faucet."

—Voice for Health

Q: How many unemployed actors does it take to change a light bulb?

A: 100. One to change it, and 99 to stand around and say, "Hey, I could've done that!"

—One to One

Q: How many economists does it take to change a light bulb?

A: How many did it take this time last year?

—The Jokesmith

Q: How many real-estate agents does it take to change a light bulb?

A: Ten. But we'll accept eight.

—BILL HOMISAK, quoted by
MARY ANN MADDEN in *New York*

Q: How many liberated women does it take to change a light bulb?

A: Five! One to turn it, and four to form a support group.

—JAY TRACHMAN in *One to One*

Q: How many surrealist painters does it take to change a light bulb?

A: A fish.

—HORACE DAVIES, quoted by
MARY ANN MADDEN in *New York*

"I'll make a deal with you. I'll tell you the secret of life if you'll tell me how to program my VCR."

Q: How many feminists does it take to change a light bulb?
A: That's not funny.

—CHRISTINA HOFF SOMMERS,
Who Stole Feminism?

Thomas Edison spent years trying to invent the electric light, testing and retesting. Finally, late one night, he got the bulb to glow. He ran out of his laboratory, through the house, up the stairs to his bedroom. "Honey," Edison called to his wife, "I've done it!"

She rolled over and said, "Will you turn off that light and come to bed!"

—RON DENTINGER in
Work Sheet

Q: How many country-western singers does it take to change a light bulb?

A: Five. One to put in the new bulb, and four to sing about how much they long for the old one.

—LESLIE R. TANNER

:) \&/HA HA!

Delbert and Fletch, two industrial robots, escaped from the engineering lab one Saturday night. They decided to separate, pick up some dates and meet later.

A few hours passed and Delbert arrived at the meeting place. He found Fletch standing in front of a mailbox and a fire alarm. "Who are your two friends?" asked Delbert.

"Forget them," sighed Fletch. "The short, fat one with the big mouth just stands there, and if you touch the redhead she screams her lungs out."

—ED MCMANUS, quoted by STEVE WOZNIAK and LARRY WILDE
in *The Official Computer Freaks Joke Book*

Mrs. B: "Why are you laughing?"
Mrs. D: "A salesman tried to sell my husband a lap-top computer."
Mrs. B: "What's so funny about that?"
Mrs. D: "My husband hasn't had a lap in 20 years!"

—YOUNG and DRAKE, King Features Syndicate

Did you hear about the new computer Apple has developed, small enough to be carried in a fanny pack? It will be called the Macintush.

—TOM CLOUD, quoted by ABIGAIL VAN BUREN,
Universal Press Syndicate

A computer salesman dies and meets St. Peter at the Pearly Gates. St. Peter tells the salesman that he can choose between heaven and hell. First he shows the man heaven, where people in white robes play harps and float around. "Dull," says the salesman.

Next, St. Peter shows him hell: toga parties, good food and wine, and people looking as though they're having a fine time. "I'll take hell," he says.

He enters the gates of hell and is immediately set upon by a dozen demons, who poke him with pitchforks. "Hey," the salesman demands as Satan walks past, "what happened to the party I saw going on?"

"Ah," Satan replies. "You must have seen our demo."

—*Digital Review*

CHIP AHOY
I bought the latest computer;
It came completely loaded.
It was guaranteed for 90 days,
But in 30 was outmoded.

—BILL IHLENFELDT in *The Wall Street Journal*

That computer you sold me is no good," complained the customer. "It keeps flashing insulting messages, like 'Look it up yourself, stupid.' "

"Oh," replied the store clerk, "you must have one of our new 'User Surly' models."

—JOHNNY HART, Creators Syndicate

The computer programmer, it seems, had allowed for every contingency. One day the operator became frustrated with her work and punched in a highly unladylike message. On the console a response immediately flashed up: "Tut, tut, improper expression."

—JANE ROUX

Q: Why is a modem better than a woman?

A: A modem doesn't complain if you sit and play at the computer all night. A modem doesn't mind if you talk to other modems. A modem will sit patiently and wait by the phone. A modem comes with an instruction manual.

—Jay Trachman in *One to One*

The exec was making a presentation to the company board. "Computers have allowed us to cut costs," he explained. "We expect even more dramatic improvements as computers become increasingly self-sufficient." He unveiled a large chart showing a man, a dog, and a computer. "Here is our organization plan of the future."

"What kind of plan is that?" demanded a board member.

"It's simple," replied the exec. "The man's job is to feed the dog. The dog's job is to bite the man if he touches the computer."

—Louis A. Mamakos

Space Invaders

Upon their return from an excursion to our planet, two Martians presented their chief with a television set. "We couldn't manage to capture any Earthlings," they explained, "but we did get our hands on one of their gods."

—Mina and André Guillois

A pair of Martians landed on a country road on Earth in the middle of the night. "Where are we?" one asked.

"I think we're in a cemetery," his companion answered. "Look at the gravestone over there—that man lived to be 108."

"What was his name?"

"Miles to Omaha."

"Take me to your remote control."

A service station attendant watching a Martian put gas into its spacecraft noticed that "UFO" was printed on the spaceship's side. "Does that stand for 'Unidentified Flying Object'?" he asked the Martian.

"No," the creature replied. " 'Unleaded Fuel Only.' "

—DELFORT D. MINOR

The White House is proposing we collaborate with Russia to build a new space station," says Jay Leno. "Know what that means? We're going to wind up with a space station that has a $30-million-dollar toilet—and no toilet paper."

The week before a space launch, an astronaut tries to relax at an out-of-the-way pub. But the bartender recognizes him and says, "You fellows at NASA think you're something, going to the moon. But we've got a couple of guys here who've been building their own spaceship out back."

Reluctantly, the astronaut goes outside to look—the spaceship is a mess of beer bottles, cans and junk. "We're planning to go to the sun," boasts one guy.

"This thing will be incinerated before you can get close to the sun," the astronaut warns.

"We got that all figured out—we're going at night!"

—HERMAN GOLLOB in *Texas Monthly*

It's the year 2210, and the planets have long been colonized. Interplanetary flight is as everyday as transcontinental flight, and on one of these interplanetary liners a Martian colonist strikes up a conversation with the passenger next to him. "Where are you from?" he asks.

"Earth," is the reply.

"Oh, really? By any chance do you know . . .?"

—MARK S. ZUELKE

"See you, Roger. I'm returning to the private sector."

Talking Animals

PET PEEVES 202
WILD THINGS 210

Pet Peeves

Is our parrot a daddy or a mommy?" asked the young boy of his mother on a crowded bus.

"She is a mommy parrot," the mother replied.

"How do we know?" the boy asked.

A hush fell over the passengers as they listened for how the mother would cope with this one. But she was ready for the challenge and replied, "She has lipstick on, hasn't she?"

—R. SARANGAPANI

The neighbor's young son came knocking at the housewife's door every day to ask if he could take her dog for a walk. Her husband, who was a carpenter, almost always took the animal with him to his jobs, so she told the child, "I'm sorry, but the dog is at work with my husband." Because the boy kept coming over every day with the same request, she always gave him the same response.

The youngster met the woman on the street one day, stopped and eyed her suspiciously. "Say," he asked, "what does your dog do for a living?"

—METTE R. NYHUS

John, teaching his parrot to talk: "Repeat after me, 'I can walk.'"

Parrot: "I can walk."

John: "I can talk."

Parrot: "I can talk."

John: "I can fly."

Parrot: "That's a lie."

—FATEH ZUNG SINGH

● ●

Overheard: "My neighbor's dog is taking the advanced course at obedience school. He knows how to fetch, heel and beg—now he's learning to fax."

—JAY TRACHMAN in *One to One*

When the farmer arrived at the obedience school to pick up his newly trained bird dog, he asked the instructor for a demonstration. The two men and the dog went to a nearby field, where the dog immediately pointed to a clump of brush, then rolled over twice.

"There are two birds in there," the instructor said, and sure enough, two birds were flushed. A minute later, the dog pointed to another bunch of bushes, and then rolled over five times.

"There are five birds in there," the instructor noted, and indeed five birds were driven from the brush. Then the dog pointed to a third clump. He began to whine and run in circles until he found a stick, which he shook mightily and dropped at the men's feet.

"And in that clump of brush there," the proud instructor concluded, "there are more birds than you can shake a stick at!"

—*Country*

Sign seen in a veterinarian's office: The doctor is in. Sit. Stay.

—GALE SHIPLEY

An agent arranged an audition with a TV producer for his client, a talking dog that told jokes and sang songs. The amazed producer was about to sign a contract when suddenly a much larger dog burst into the room, grabbed the talking pooch by the neck and bounded back out.

"What happened?" demanded the producer.

"That's his mother," said the agent. "She wants him to be a doctor."

—*Cheer*

Overheard at the veterinarian's: "I had my cat neutered. He's still out all night with the other cats, but now it's in the role of consultant."

—*Current Comedy*

Walking down the street, a dog saw a sign in an office window. "Help wanted. Must type 70 words a minute. Must be computer literate. Must be bilingual. An equal-opportunity employer."

The dog applied for the position, but he was quickly rebuffed. "I can't hire a dog for this job," the office manager said. But when the dog pointed to the line that read "An equal-opportunity employer," the office manager sighed and asked, "Can you type?" Silently, the dog walked over to a typewriter and flawlessly banged out a letter. "Can you operate a computer?" the manager inquired. The dog then sat down at a terminal, wrote a program and ran it perfectly.

"Look, I still can't hire a dog for this position," said the exasperated office manager. "You have fine skills, but I need someone who's bilingual. It says so right in the ad."

The dog looked up at the manager and said, "Meow."

—DONALD WEINSTEIN, quoted by LAWRENCE VAN GELDER
in *The New York Times*

A dog goes into the unemployment office and asks for help finding a job. "With your rare talent," says the clerk, "I'm sure we can get you something at the circus."

"The circus?" echoes the dog. "What would a circus want with a plumber?"

—JAY TRACHMAN in *One to One*

Did you hear about the cat that gave birth in a Singapore street? It got fined for littering.

—DAWN FUNG

"Have you noticed how Ed has changed since he started going to law school?"

Please keep your dog beside you, sir," a woman said crossly to the man sitting opposite her on the bus. "I can feel a flea in my shoe."

"Bello, come here," replied the man. "That woman has fleas."

—J. G.

Mrs. Klapisch brought her cat to the veterinarian. The doctor had her hold the animal on the examining table as he touched and gently squeezed it. He then walked slowly around the table, all the while looking back and forth, back and forth. When he was done, he gave out some medication and presented Mrs. Klapisch with the bill.

"What?" she cried. "One hundred fifty dollars for two pills?"

"Not just for pills," said the vet. "I gave her a cat scan too."

—David W. Fleeton

Henry's new job had him spending a lot of time on the road, and out of concern for his wife's safety he visited a pet shop to look at watchdogs.

"I have just the dog for you," said the salesman, showing him a miniature Pekingese.

"Come on," Henry protested, "that little thing couldn't hurt a flea."

"Ah, but he knows karate," the salesman replied. "Here, let me show you." He pointed to a cardboard box and ordered, "Karate the box!" Immediately the dog shredded it. The salesman then pointed to an old wooden chair and instructed, "Karate the chair!" The dog reduced the chair to matchsticks. Astounded, Henry bought the dog.

When he got home, Henry announced that he had purchased a watchdog, but his wife took one look at the Pekingese and was unimpressed. "That scrawny thing couldn't fight his way out of a paper bag!" she said.

"But this Pekingese is special," Henry insisted. "He's a karate expert."

"Now I've heard everything," Helen replied. "Karate my foot!"

—JIM ELLSWORTH

Several racehorses are in a stable. One of them starts boasting about his track record.

"Of my last 15 races," he says, "I've won eight."

Another horse breaks in, "Well, I've won 19 of my last 27!"

"That's good, but I've taken 28 of 36," says another, flicking his tail.

At this point a greyhound who's been sitting nearby pipes up. "I don't mean to boast," he says, "but of my last 90 races, I've won 88."

The horses are clearly amazed. "Wow," says one after a prolonged silence, "a talking dog!"

—PETER S. LANGSTON

"I'm really worried about my dog," Ralph said to the veterinarian. "I dropped some coins on the floor and before I could pick them up, he ate them." The vet advised Ralph to leave his dog at the vet's office overnight.

The next morning, Ralph called to see how his pet was doing. The vet replied, "No change yet."

—MIKE WALT, SR.

The pet-shop customer couldn't believe his good fortune. The parrot he had just bought could recite Shakespeare's sonnets, imitate opera stars and intone Homer's epic poems in Greek. And he cost only $600.

Once the man got the bird home, however, not another word passed his beak. After three weeks the disconsolate customer returned to the shop and asked for his money back. "When we had this bird," said the proprietor, "he could recite poetry and sing like an angel. Now you want me to take him back when he's no longer himself? Well, all right. Out of the goodness of my heart I'll give you $100."

Reluctantly the man accepted his loss. Just as the door shut behind him he heard the parrot say to the shop owner, "Don't forget—my share is $250."

—C. A. HENDERSON

A man answered his doorbell, and a friend walked in, followed by a very large dog. As they began talking, the dog knocked over a lamp, jumped on the sofa with his muddy paws and began chewing a pillow. The outraged householder, unable to contain himself any longer, burst out, "Can't you control your dog better?"

"*My* dog!" exclaimed the friend. "I thought it was *your* dog."

—*The Great Clean Jokes Calendar*

"I'm sick and tired of begging."

A man trained his dog to go around the corner to Bud's Lounge every day with two dollar bills under his collar to get a pack of cigarettes. Once the man only had a five, so he put it under the collar and sent the dog on his way.

An hour passed and the pooch still hadn't returned. So the man went to Bud's and found his dog sitting on a bar stool, drinking a beer. He said, "You've never done this before."

Replied the dog, "I never had the money before."

—GARRISON KEILLOR, *We Are Still Married*

A guy walks into a bar and orders a beer. "Listen," he says to the bartender. "If I show you the most amazing thing you've ever seen, is my beer on the house?"

"We'll see," says the bartender. So the guy pulls a hamster and a tiny piano out of a bag, puts them on the bar, and the hamster begins to play. "Impressive," says the bartender, "but I'll need to see more."

"Hold on," says the man. He then pulls out a bullfrog, and it sings "Old Man River." A patron jumps up from his table and shouts, "That's absolutely incredible! I'll give you $100 right now for the frog."

"Sold," says the guy. The other patron takes the bullfrog and leaves.

"It's none of my business," says the bartender, "but you just gave away a fortune."

"Not really," says the guy. "The hamster is also a ventriloquist."

—ANDY BALE, WHUD, Peekskill, N.Y.

A man went to the movies and was surprised to find a woman with a big collie sitting in front of him. Even more amazing was the fact that the dog always laughed in the right places through the comedy.

"Excuse me," the man said to the woman, "but I think it's astounding that your dog enjoys the movie so much."

"I'm surprised myself," she replied. "He hated the book."

—GRAHAM FOSTER in Tomahawk, Wis., *Leader,* quoted by DEBBIE CHRISTIAN in the Milwaukee *Journal*

Kerry the tomcat was scampering all over the neighborhood—down alleys, up fire escapes, into cellars. A disturbed neighbor knocked on the owner's door and said, "Your cat is rushing about like mad."

"I know," the man conceded. "Kerry's just been neutered, and he's running around canceling engagements."

—LARRY WILDE, *Library of Laughter*

Wild Things

A forest ranger, trekking through a remote campground area, caught a whiff of something burning in the distance. Farther along the trail he found an old hermit making his evening meal.

"What are you cooking?" the ranger asked.

"Peregrine falcon," answered the hermit.

"*Peregrine falcon!*" the conservationist said, shocked. "You can't cook that! It's on the endangered species list."

"How was I to know?" the hermit questioned. "I haven't had contact with the outside world in ages."

The ranger told the recluse he wouldn't report him this time, but he wasn't to cook peregrine falcon ever again. "By the way," he asked, "what does it taste like?"

"Well," replied the hermit, "I'd say it's somewhere between a dodo bird and a whooping crane."

—RICHARD SCHULDt, quoted by Alex Thien
in the Milwaukee *Sentinel*

A father took his children to the zoo. All were looking forward to seeing the monkeys. Unfortunately, it was mating time and, the attendant explained, the monkeys had gone inside their little sanctuary for some togetherness. "Would they come out for some peanuts?" asked the father.

"Would you?" responded the attendant.

—CHARLEY MANOS in *The Detroit News*

When a snail crossed the road, he was run over by a turtle. Regaining consciousness in the emergency room, he was asked what caused the accident.

"I really can't remember," the snail replied. "You see, it all happened so fast."

—CHARLES MCMANIS

"I don't know why I even made this trip—I'm not even sexually active."

The photographer had been trying for hours to get some action shots of a bear that preferred to sleep in its cage. "What kind of bear is that?" he finally asked the zoo keeper.

"Himalayan," was the reply.

"I know that," snarled the photographer. "What I want to know is when him a getting up."

—RICHARD A. UECKER

The zoo built a special eight-foot-high enclosure for its newly acquired kangaroo, but the next morning the animal was found hopping around outside. The height of the fence was increased to 15 feet, but the kangaroo got out again. Exasperated, the zoo director had the height increased to 30 feet, but the kangaroo still escaped. A giraffe asked the kangaroo, "How high do you think they'll build the fence?"

"I don't know," said the kangaroo. "Maybe a thousand feet if they keep leaving the gate unlocked."

—JERRY H. SIMPSON, JR.

A woman lion tamer had the big cats under such control they took a lump of sugar from her lips on command. "Anyone can do that!" a skeptic yelled.

The ringmaster came over and asked, "Would you like to try it?"

"Sure," replied the man, "but first get those crazy lions out of there!"

—*Healthwise*

A rooster was strutting around the henhouse one Easter morning and came across a nest of eggs dyed every color of the rainbow. The rooster took one look at the colorful display, ran outside and beat the heck out of the resident peacock.

—SEYMOUR ROSENBERG in the
Spartanburg, S.C., *Herald-Journal*

As spring migration approached, two elderly vultures doubted they could make the trip north, so they decided to go by airplane.

When they checked their baggage, the attendant noticed that they were carrying two dead armadillos. "Do you wish to check the armadillos through as luggage?" she asked.

"No, thanks," replied the vultures. "They're carrion."

—FRED BRICE

The old big-game hunter is recounting his adventures to his grandson:

"I remember, I once had to brave eight ferocious lions with no gun, nothing but a knife to defend me. My life was at stake. . . ."

"Granddad, the last time you told this story, there were only three lions!"

"Yes, but then you were too young to hear the terrible truth."

—ADAM WOLFART

Did you hear about the scientist who crossed a carrier pigeon with a woodpecker?

He got a bird that not only delivers messages to their destination but knocks on the door when it gets there.

—JOHN R. FOX

An antelope and a lion entered a diner and took a booth near the window. When the waiter approached, the antelope said, "I'll have a bowl of hay and a side order of radishes."

"And what will your friend have?"

"Nothing," replied the antelope.

The waiter persisted. "Isn't he hungry?"

"Hey, if he were hungry," said the antelope, "would I be sitting here?"

—*Current Comedy*

An expert on whales was telling friends about some of the unusual findings he had made. "For instance," he said, "some whales can communicate at a distance of 300 miles."

"What on earth would one whale say to another 300 miles away?" asked an astounded member of the group.

"I'm not absolutely sure," answered the expert, "but it sounds something like 'Can you still hear me?' "

—STEVE KEUCHEL

"Forgive me? It must have been the beast in me talking."

We have a skunk in the basement," shrieked the caller to the police dispatcher. "How can we get it out?"

"Take some bread crumbs," said the dispatcher, "and put down a trail from the basement out to the backyard. Then leave the cellar door open."

Sometime later the resident called back. "Did you get rid of it?" asked the dispatcher.

"No," replied the caller. "Now I have two skunks in there!"

—*Ohio Motorist*

....

And then there was the male spotted owl who told his wife, "What do you mean you have a headache? We're an endangered species!"

—JOHN BUNZEL, quoted by HERB CAEN
in the San Francisco *Chronicle*

While drinking at the lake, a young bear admires its reflection and growls, "I am the king of beasts!"

Along comes a lion and roars, "What was that I just heard?"

"Oh, dear," says the bear, "you say strange things when you've had too much to drink."

—LEA BERNER

Dad," a polar bear cub asked his father, "am I 100 percent polar bear?"

"Of course you are," answered the elder bear. "My parents are 100 percent polar bear, which makes me 100 percent polar bear. Your mother's parents are all polar bear, so she's 100 percent polar bear. Yep, that makes you 100 percent polar bear too. Why do you want to know?"

Replied the cub, " 'Cause I'm freezing!"

—"T & T," KCYY, San Antonio

A male crab met a female crab and asked her to marry him. She noticed that he was walking straight instead of sideways. *Wow,* she thought, *this crab is really special. I can't let him get away.* So they got married immediately.

The next day she noticed her new husband walking sideways like all the other crabs, and got upset. "What happened?" she asked. "You used to walk straight before we were married."

"Oh, honey," he replied, "I can't drink that much every day."

—GITY KAZEMIAN

TALKING ANIMALS